Going Freelance

Going Freelance

Stuart Derrick

crimson

Startups: Going Freelance
This first edition published in 2012 by Crimson Publishing Ltd, Westminster House,
Kew Road, Richmond, Surrey TW9 2ND

Author: Stuart Derrick

British Library Cataloguing in Publication Data
A catalogue record for this book is available from the British Library

ISBN 978 1 85458 672 8

Designed by Andy Prior
Typeset by IDSUK (DataConnection) Ltd
Printed and bound in the UK by Ashford Colour Press, Gosport, Hants

Contents

Contents

Introduction

The 9 to 5 life isn't for everyone. A growing number of people are looking to pursue a freelance career, where they take their skills and work for an interesting range of clients of their choosing. It represents a break from the comfortable, and maybe slightly stultifying, traditional career of working for 'the man' and taking home a salary at the end of the month.

Some people make the decision for themselves, while an increasing number are finding that freelancing presents the best opportunity to make a living in a working world where there are fewer and fewer certainties. There are few sectors where you can readily count on a job for life anymore. As well as the nature of work changing, we have different expectations for our working lives, with the concept of work–life balance now something that many of us are on nodding acquaintance with.

Freelance body PCG has estimated that the number of freelancers in the UK is anywhere between 1.4 million and 4 million (depending on the definition of a freelance worker used). In the report *Defining and Estimating the Size of the Freelance Workforce*, PCG went on to assert that freelancers were responsible for generating 8% of private sector turnover – £222bn.

However, for anybody starting off on a freelance career, such encouraging statistics can seem a long way from the reality of their experience. Working for yourself can be a lonely and frightening experience initially – even seasoned freelance pros will admit to waking in a cold sweat at the prospect of a looming deadline or not having enough work.

Being a freelancer is unlike many jobs, because it requires a much larger portfolio of skills than you might need when working in a traditional company set up. You really have to be a jack of all trades, and hopefully the master of one that companies will actually want to pay you for. As well as your core competence, you will need to become an accomplished marketer and salesperson, an administrator, IT fixer, financial whizz kid and chief tea and coffee maker.

No one becomes the finished article overnight. It can take years to develop the skills that will make you a successful freelancer and keep you top of the contact list for work opportunities. And that is where this book comes in.

Going Freelance is a hands-on guide to the practicalities of setting yourself up as a freelancer, and includes real advice from real freelancers on different aspects of what it takes to make a success of your new career.

It breaks down the process of becoming a freelancer and sustaining a career into easy to understand sections. Each chapter begins with a handy summary of what will be covered and concludes with a checklist of what to do next.

The book kicks off with the question of whether freelancing really is the right choice for you. It isn't for everyone, but what should you weigh up before arriving at your decision? And how do you decide if you have the right personality for freelancing in the first place? This book will help you decide for yourself if you are freelance material by looking at the pros and cons of working for yourself.

Once you have made the decision to go freelance, what do you do next? Chapter 2 will take you through the various stages from informing your erstwhile employer, and registering as self-employed, to understanding the various rules and regulations that may affect you.

Deciding what freelance career to pursue is crucially important. There are many jobs that are suited to working in a freelance capacity, from such favourites as journalist and designer, to more specialist options such as translation and tuition. Chapter 3 takes an in-depth look at some of the more popular options and explains what's involved in freelancing in these fields, how you can get started, tools of the trade and any qualifications that might be necessary or useful. It also covers the important issue of where you can get work.

Many freelancers work from home, so Chapter 4 explains how to create a home office with a working environment that encourages maximum productivity. As well as explaining the kit that you need, it looks at the best way to create the right environment for working. Office distractions can be swapped for home-based ones such as demanding family members, the TV, or the lure of some other pressing task that drags you away from work.

Staying focused is just one of the challenges in managing your new career. Finding and maintaining a steady flow of work can be one of the toughest, and is one that you will have to master. Learning how to pitch ideas to achieve new commissions is a key new skill to develop and Chapter 5 gives useful tips on how to do it. As a freelancer, you have to think of yourself as a mini-business and take into account important considerations such as how to become a reliable supplier. There is plenty of advice on other skills such as time management, successful networking and pricing your work. It even covers the troublesome issue of how to ask for a raise.

For any business, there's no escape from admin, and freelancing is no different, so Chapter 6 concludes by examining the importance of staying on top of invoicing, getting paid, expenses and filing tax returns. It's probably not what you became a freelancer to do, but getting it right can be as significant as delivering a good piece of work to a client.

Deciding to become a freelancer can be one of the most exciting decisions you will ever make. There is no doubt that for many people it offers a more flexible, satisfying and interesting way to work. For those with families, it can help provide a greater amount of time to be around your children when they are growing up, which is something that more and more people are looking for. For others, it is all about doing something more creative with their lives or achieving a greater sense of control.

Whatever the motivation, at the end of the day, freelancing is a job like any other, albeit one that requires a slightly different set of skills. It can take some time to develop all the assets you need to become a great freelancer. *Going Freelance* aims to help you to hit the ground running by covering the key 'need to know' issues.

Good luck with your new career. Now what are you waiting for?

↩ *CHAPTER 1*
What to consider

 **What's in this chapter?**

Becoming a freelancer can mark an exciting career change, but before taking the plunge you need to think carefully about what it entails. What are your motivations for going freelance? Are you suited to the freelance life? Will you be able to earn enough in your new career choice?

These are just some of the questions you should try to answer before making your decision. This chapter will help you decide whether you're a freelancer at heart by looking at:

→ *what is freelancing?*
→ *will you be suited to freelancing?*
→ *what will the set-up costs be?*
→ *how much can you earn?*

Why go freelance?

For an increasing number of people, the question is not 'Why go freelance?' but 'Why not?' If you are working for an unappreciative boss, in a workplace that you don't like, doing work that you find unappealing, for a salary that doesn't seem a fair recognition of your worth, why wouldn't you want to find another way?

Freelancing promises a break from most of the downsides associated with traditional ways of working. As your own boss you may be able to find more interesting and varied work, work from home or in a range of more stimulating environments, and earn more money into the bargain.

It's a way of working that is becoming increasingly common. The jobs market has been changing rapidly over the last few years and increasing numbers of companies now use freelancers to cover specialist tasks, staff shortages and holiday periods instead of taking on full-time employees. There has never been a better time to consider being a freelancer.

Economic downturn

For some people, the choice to become a freelancer is one that they will not have made willingly. As businesses and organisations undergo restructuring, resulting in job losses, some people will find themselves forced into freelancing as a way of filling the gap until the next job comes along.

The good news is that you needn't panic. Many jobs are now able to be done in a freelance capacity, and whether you are forced to be a freelancer or become one as a positive lifestyle choice, the opportunities to do well are fantastic ... if you go about planning your new career in the right way.

Career opportunities

You should think of freelancing as a career. Too many people start freelancing with vague ideas that it will allow them to devote time to other interests in life, whether it be visiting art galleries, learning a foreign language, or simply having more time to travel.

Stop and think again. Freelancing can be as hard as any other job. In the early days, when you are struggling to establish yourself, it may be even harder as you work all hours to fulfil commitments and are fearful of turning down work.

With rising unemployment, there are now more candidates than ever for any full-time job that is advertised, and the same goes for freelancing. Unless you are lucky enough to be considered the country's sole expert on a particularly niche and highly paid field, the world is not likely to beat a path to your door and offer you work. You will have to compete against other, equally hungry freelancers, who may have similar or better skills to you, and who are after the same work.

Being a freelancer is a job like any other. The key to successful freelancing is to be professional, respect deadlines, never take commissions or clients for granted and to always be on the lookout for the next job.

Apart from that, it's easy.

What is freelancing?

The term 'freelance' originates from a time when mercenary soldiers would offer their services to the highest bidder. These 'free lances' would move from job to job, and were tied to no single employer.

Today the term 'freelance' describes professionals who are similarly free to work with anyone. A freelancer is a self-employed person with a particular skill such as writing, teaching, IT or public relations. They do exactly the same job as an in-house employee and are paid either at an hourly rate or a fixed project fee.

Businesses like them because they are the ultimate flexible resource that they can use on a short-term, as-needed basis to fill a gap.

Because freelancers are self-employed, they avoid the hidden and expensive employment costs, such as National Insurance, pension contributions, sickness payments, and any of the other benefits that businesses offer to full timers.

This means that freelancers can generally charge a premium because of their flexibility and their lower employment costs.

Freelancers can also work for a range of companies at once, so if your time management is good, you can be more productive and more highly paid as you fit more work into the available working day. By spreading your workload around several different companies, you may also ride out the ups and downs of the economic cycle a bit better as you are unlikely to be made redundant by all of them.

Jobs that can be done as a freelancer

There are plenty of jobs that can be done on a freelance basis. Here are just a few of them:

- actor
- advertising executive
- advisor
- cartoonist
- chef
- children's entertainer
- consultant
- designer
- editor
- film maker
- gardener
- illustrator
- IT contractor
- market researcher
- musician
- party or event planner
- PR person
- project manager
- proof reader
- salesperson
- teacher or tutor
- therapist
- translator
- website manager
- writer or journalist.

Freelancer or contractor?

The terms 'freelancer' and 'contractor' can be used interchangeably, but they are subtly different.

Freelancers tend to work with many different clients on a variety of projects. They are responsible for finding their own work and looking after their own records, such as invoicing, books and tax returns.

Contractors resemble freelancers inasmuch as they are not generally looking for full-time permanent roles. They tend to look for fixed-term work contracts, which can involve working with one employer for anything from a few days to a few months. They may take on bigger pieces of work, and may be more likely to work from a client's office for the duration of the contract.

The distinctions between the two are subtle, but generally speaking, a contractor will work exclusively and full time for a client for a specified period of time. Generally, this will be at a client's place of work. Contractors are common in the IT industry in particular.

By contrast, a freelancer will have a portfolio of clients that they work for, and will often work from home. The bonds between freelancer and client are much looser and either party can effectively decide to terminate their arrangement at any time. This is a common model across media sectors.

However, there is a crossover between the two descriptions. Some freelancers welcome the security of taking on a contract for a short period of time. However, if security becomes an overriding concern, you may want to reconsider your freelance status and look for a full-time salaried position. Contractors can also freelance in between contracts – so it's often difficult to tell the difference between the two.

Who does it suit?

More money, more varied work, and more control over your working life. Who wouldn't want to be a freelancer? Freelancing sounds very attractive, but these advantages are just one side of the equation. Setting aside the fact that some people may be forced by economic necessity into freelancing, it doesn't suit everybody.

Whether you are doing a bit of freelancing on the side of your main job or making freelancing your new full-time occupation, there are a few things that you should bear in mind. Don't be completely seduced by the upside, because there is also an accompanying downside.

Freelancing differs from a full-time salaried job in a number of respects, not least the fact that there is no longer the comfort of a salary miraculously popping into your bank account at the end of the month. You have to find your own work, deliver to exacting deadlines, work out what you are going to charge for work, and keep that supply of work coming in.

There are also a lot of plates to spin. As a freelancer, you are effectively a one-person corporation. So, as well as actually doing the work, you need to be:

→ the marketing person raising awareness of your skills and availability

→ the salesperson, who converts that interest into paid work

→ the accounts department, which generates the invoices, chases payment and deals with your accounts and tax returns, and don't forget VAT. If you have outgoings, you will also have to deal with payments to your suppliers

→ the client services person who liaises with clients to ensure a smooth working relationship

→ the IT department when your computer goes on the blink

→ the office cleaner at the end of the day.

You will also be responsible for such issues as training and making sure your skills are up to date, and any general administration that would have been handled by somebody else in a bigger company. Once you are out on your own there is no longer the shelter of senior employees to correct your mistakes or cover your faults. For this reason, freelancers are typically well rounded in their skills.

To be a successful freelancer, it is also helpful if you are already established to a certain extent in your sector. In some sectors, such as journalism, it is not impossible to begin your career freelancing but it is a tough start. With some experience behind you, your contact book will be better able to deliver work for you. A good track record makes it simpler to get work as people will already know what you are capable of and will trust you.

So, is freelancing for you? Here are some things to bear in mind before making that decision.

Finding work

As companies make redundancies and restructure to leaner, meaner operations, there is a lot of freelance work out there as companies look to outsource more work. But getting a job is a job in itself. Think carefully about where your work is likely to come from. Will there be enough of it and will it be regular enough? What will it pay? As well as existing contacts, you will need to market yourself a bit more and let people know about what you can do. What will your strategy be?

Your skills

Do you have skills or experience that others require? The more in-demand your skills are, the more work you will generate and the higher the fees you will command. This is why it is often better to embark on a freelance career later in your career. Clients use freelancers where they have a skills gap of their own, and it's more likely that somebody with a packed CV is going to be in demand than a new starter.

Will you earn enough?

Take a close look at what you need to earn in a given month and try to honestly assess whether you can earn that through freelancing. Day rates for freelancing may sound fantastic as a pro rata calculation, but what about the days when you are not needed? Also, work into your calculations how you will fund holidays, illness and other downtime.

Limit your own pay

Remember that there is a difference between what you need to earn and what you want to earn. As a full-time salaried person, you will have got used to being paid a set amount every month, and you will probably spend all of it by the next payday. As a freelancer, the equation switches. There is no set pay for the month, and it is a good discipline to pay yourself what you can get by on and set the rest aside for a rainy day. As a freelancer, some days are more rainy than others.

Payment gaps

A month can seem a long time as you try and eke out your salary, but imagine waiting several months for payment at a time when your own bills are mounting up. Different clients have different payment policies, but periods of 60 or 90 days from the production of an invoice are not uncommon. It can also depend on when your work is published – some publishers only stump up after a magazine or newspaper hits the streets and you may have been commissioned weeks in advance. For these reasons, you will need to have some reserves to tide you over. Many freelancers look to have at least three months of salary in reserve, although six will put you in a more secure position. See p. 203 for more on methods for managing your finances.

Deadlines, deadlines

Although freelancing may seem to promise to free you from the 9 to 5 rat race to a certain extent, you are still prey to the demands of your clients. You may decide to spend your daytime hours watching art house movies or visiting museums, and working into the night, but ultimately the project needs to be delivered. Freelancing is also a numbers game to a certain extent. The more work you do, the more you get paid, so hitting those deadlines is not only good for your reputation, it allows you to cram in more assignments. If you are the sort of person who will use up all the available time to complete a project, freelancing may not be for you.

Time management

People who freelance have to be realistic about the amount of work they can take on. It can be seductive to look at the fee for a project and have it mentally spent before you've done the work. Consider how you are going to be able to do it and what effect that will have on your health, family life and sanity. Don't overburden yourself.

Marketing yourself

Clients will judge you on the quality of your previous work as much as recommendations from others. Work out how you will present the best version of yourself. Do you need a portfolio? Can you point to examples of your work online? Do you have your own website or blog?

Are you a jack of all trades?

You no longer have the back-up of working in a larger organisation. The most senior person finds themselves doing their own filing, not to mention making their own tea. More importantly, if you're used to working within a managed or supervised environment, it can be a shock to find that you make all the decisions and set timelines. You may not have all the skills that you need at first, so are you prepared to pick them up?

Can you pull an all-nighter?

There are times when a pressing deadline will mean you have to work around the clock to complete the job on time. The nature of freelancing can be feast or famine, and it's often a case of having to work when the work is available and catching up on your sleep when you can. Flexibility is important, and who knows, next week you may have no paid work at all.

Are you a lone wolf?

Rather than the social environment of an office, many freelancers can find themselves working at home alone. Although this can mean you will skip lots of interruptions such as colleagues discussing what was on TV last night, you also miss out on essential office scuttlebutt. Social media can make working remotely or alone less isolating, but it is something that may not suit everybody.

How much can you earn?

How long is a piece of string?

Earnings as a freelancer will depend on a number of factors.

→ **Your work rate:** to a certain extent, freelancing is a numbers game. The more work you do, the more you get paid. If you are a fast, reliable freelancer, then you can get through more work.

→ **Your rate:** every freelancer will be paid slightly differently. This will depend on their skills and experience, their specialisations, and their own bargaining powers. Employers never want to pay you what you think you are worth, and you can either meekly accept their rates or make the case why you are worth more. Your rate may also reflect the urgency of a particular piece of work. If something is required to a short deadline, there should be a premium that reflects that you may have to put other things on hold and burn the midnight oil to get the work out on time.

→ **Seniority:** the further up the job ladder you are in your particular sector, the more you can earn. However, individual jobs may be harder to come by in more senior positions, so you may find that seniority in itself does not guarantee higher earnings. You may have to drop down a level or two to guarantee work.

→ **Type of work:** some work is more valued than others and the rates will reflect this. If you are churning out listings all day, you shouldn't expect to be earning the same rate as a freelance analyst studying complex oil and gas prices and producing a hard-hitting report for a client.

→ **Supply and demand:** if you operate in a sector that is heavily subscribed, rates will be depressed. A classic example is that of music magazines where there are a huge number of eager music fans trying to get into print, often for the love of music and for the glory of seeing their name in print. If people will work for free, don't expect the pay to be great.

→ **The economy:** in a downturn, freelance rates can plummet as clients are less prepared to pay the going rate, and there is an increase in supply.

→ **Where your work is used:** for writers and photographers, the higher profile and the bigger the circulation, the more you can charge. A picture for *Tractors Monthly* may pay you a couple of hundred pounds, but an advertising shoot for a fashion brand could lead to a payment in the thousands.

Pay rates will vary for freelancers within industries as well as across different sectors. However, it is fair to say that there is potential to earn more money as a freelancer than doing the same job as a staff member.

The reasons are simple. Because employers don't have to pay National Insurance, holiday pay and various staff benefits to freelancers, they can afford, and indeed expect, to pay a bit more to freelancers. Also, because they only use a freelance resource when they need it, the cost need not become prohibitive.

Freelance rates can seem enticing for some people stuck in a staff job. If the day rate for freelancers is £200, then that equates to £52,000 a year. For someone who may be on half that amount, it's tempting to see freelancing as an enticing alternative career path.

Of course it's not as simple as that. It's unlikely that you will be working all of the time – otherwise the employer would be better off having somebody being paid less on their staff. Full-time staff have benefits that freelancers have to sort out for themselves, such as paid holiday and sick leave.

Remember to take your holidays into account when calculating your potential income for the year. If you plan to take five weeks' holiday in the first year, this will cut nearly 10% off your annual income.

You also have to deduct various costs – say, telephone, fax and computer use at £20 for the week, research materials such as magazines and reports at £10 per week, stationery, postage and other expenses at £10 a week, plus an allowance of £30 a week for travel costs for meeting people, getting new commissions, and so on. Before you start out, it is a good idea to do a rough estimation of what you need to live on each month. Sit down and work out all of your outgoings for a month: rent, utilities, transport, childcare, subsistence, insurance, and so on and figure how much you will need to earn to cover that amount.

Another very important issue in freelance earnings is to be disciplined about putting money aside for the taxman. You are now responsible for your own tax affairs and it can be tempting to put all your earnings into a pot labelled 'Mine'. Make sure you deduct enough for tax or you could suddenly find yourself short.

Some real rates

It is notoriously difficult to get hold of rates for freelancing, precisely because they are so fluid and because people set their own rates of pay. For aspiring freelancers, the best thing to do can be to take a straw poll of what people are being paid. Speak to freelancers that you know and find out what they charge and why. Also speak to anybody at your current employers who has used freelancers and find out what they are willing to pay for particular job types.

You can also speak to specialist recruitment companies who act for freelancers and ask them about current rates. Bear in mind that the rates paid by agencies will probably be below what you could earn yourself if you forged a direct relationship with an employer, as agencies will take a hefty commission fee before paying you.

Finally, go online to job forums and interest groups and find out what people are being paid. Bear in mind that what some people think is good money won't be enough to get others out of bed in the morning.

The National Union of Journalists (NUJ) produces an excellent guide to what freelancers can earn, which is listed online at www.londonfreelance.org/feesguide.

Of particular note is the wide variety of pay rates in each sector. The NUJ points out that different parts of the media tend to operate around different norms. Book publishing, for example, usually pays less than national newspapers – although not always. Some rates, such as photography for national newspapers, seem to be fairly consistent, while in others, such as magazines, there are huge variations between different publications.

Example rates

Broadcasting (BBC)
- Walk and talk: £110
- Day rate reporting: £241
- DV feature shot and edited on own equipment: £1,182

Books
- Writing and researching: £275 per 1,000 words
- Copy editing: £24 per hour
- Picture editing: £22 per hour
- Proofreading: £21 per hour

Magazines
- Reporting shift: £140–£220 per day depending on size of title
- Acting as editor: £180–£350 per day depending on size of title
- Writing, per 1,000 words: £250–£500+ per day depending on size of title
- Subediting/production: £140–£200 per day

National newspapers
- News shift: £170–£180 per day
- Sub-editing: £150–£290

PR
- In-house press officer: £220–£330
- Monthly retainer: £1,200–£2,400
- Consultancy: £320–£500 per day

Photography
- Half day rate for magazines: £175–£300 depending on size of title
- Day rate: £300–£800 depending on size of title
- Corporate rates: £800–£2,000
    Source: *Freelance fees guide* www.londonfreelance.org/feesguide.

Advertising
- Junior art director: £100–£150
- Senior art director: £200–£350+
- Copywriters: £180–£400
- Account director: £180–£300
- Senior planner: £250–£800
    Source: Day rates from Xchangeteam; www.xchangeteam.com.
See www.xchangeteam.com/freelance-example-rates for a full range of example rates.

What's your rate?

Consider the rates that you can realistically expect to be paid, and calculate how much work you will have to do each month to cover your costs. Is it realistic? Can you attract that amount of work, and can you actually do it in the time that you will have available for work? If not, then you'll have to revisit the sums and see where adjustments can be made. Can you trim your costs? Is there a way of getting a higher rate for your work? Can you work more hours? Is there another income stream that you may have overlooked, such as licensing your work to another organisation?

Will you make enough?

There is one final thing to bear in mind. If financial concerns are your main worry, then you should think long and hard about whether freelancing it the right option for you. Yes, the opportunity is there to make more than you would as a salaried employee. However, that opportunity is contingent on many variables that may be outside of your control, not least the amount of work that is available at any one time.

Work can be seasonal. Freelance copywriting work, as an example, often falls away in the summer and at Christmas when fewer marketing campaigns are run. Freelance children's entertainers tend to have less work in the summer too, but more in the run-up to Christmas.

Anybody who tells you that being a freelancer is the road to riches is pulling your leg.

How much does it cost?

Many freelancers work from home so the start-up costs are minimal – a bedroom converted to an office, with a desk, computer and internet access, a telephone and an answering machine. You may also need business stationery and business cards for advertising yourself to clients. You may even wish to produce brochures about your services too.

As a rule of thumb, you could be looking at £1,000–£1,500 to set yourself up properly at home. It doesn't pay to skimp on the tools of your trade. Buying a second-hand laptop will seem a false economy if it crashes halfway through an important project and you haven't backed up your material elsewhere.

Not everybody who wants to is able to work from home. You may have children and find it too distracting or simply too crowded working at home. It is possible to rent desk space in a shared office. You may be able to rent a desk from £50 a week, which could include phone and internet access, and might even bundle in IT support. It can also be more appealing for some freelancers to work in a setting with other people, rather than on their own. See pp 83-86 for more information on the costs of setting up a home office.

Tools of the trade

Set-up costs will vary depending on the type of work you are carrying out. For some freelancers, such as a freelance photographer or cameraman, a car may be a necessity to get from job to job. Designers may find that they need to invest in a more pricey Apple computer, rather than making do with a more generic laptop that a writer could get away with. And then there is the cost of programs such as Photoshop and InDesign on top of this.

You may have some tools of your particular trade to buy as well. A freelance music teacher needs instruments and a freelance children's entertainer requires costumes and props. For many freelancers, such as PR consultants, writers and proofreaders, there are few other expenses. Sometimes, freelancers are asked to work on the client's premises so that they are close to where the action is.

However, it pays to remember that this is all investment for your chosen career and you will be able to put much of it against your tax bill at year end.

 Checklist

- ☑ Consider your motivations for going freelance in the first place. Are you fully committed to doing what it takes to make a go of it?

- ☑ Are you suited to being a freelancer? What skills and experience do you have that could help you build a successful freelance career?

- ☑ Speak to other freelancers to get a full picture of what it is really like to freelance.

Checklist

☑ Will you freelance full time from the beginning, or can you freelance from your existing job to gradually build a portfolio of work contacts?

☑ Look at the going rates for work in your sector and then assess what you will be able to charge and how much work you can realistically accomplish.

☑ Look at how much you need to earn a month to get by.

☑ What sum of money will you need to invest to get you started? Remember to build in a sum for the first few months before money starts to trickle in.

CHAPTER 2

Popular freelance careers

📖 What's in this chapter?

There are many jobs that freelancers can do. Each one is different, but there are commonalities to all of them. In this chapter we will examine some freelance jobs and look in detail at what you need to be successful in them. We'll look at:

→ *getting started*
→ *tools of the trade*
→ *qualifications*
→ *where you can get work.*

How to become a freelance writer

In some ways, it has never been a better time to become a freelance writer. Although the death of print is always much anticipated, there are probably more niche magazines, newspapers and journals being printed than ever before. And that's before you start to consider the massive growth in online publications and websites that require content.

The barriers to entry are relatively low, in that anybody with a good idea for an article can theoretically see it end up in print – on- or offline – if they go about things the right way. There are plenty of examples of box-fresh writers successfully pitching ideas to national newspapers and magazines. Given publications' constant need to interest their readers with something new and exciting, new writers may even be at an advantage, as they are more likely to come up with novel ideas than tired old hacks.

The flip side is that there is more competition than ever in the writing arena. Just as everyone probably has a novel in them, everybody has a handful of good features ideas in them. To be a consistently successful writer requires dedication, hard work and enthusiasm.

Getting started

It's never too early to start writing, whether it be for a school newspaper, an association newsletter or a newsstand magazine; the disciplines required are the same for each of them. Even if this work is unpaid – and most writers will have to work for nothing at the start of their careers to gain work experience – it will allow you to build up a portfolio of cuttings. Throughout your writing career, this will be one of the most important tools for gaining more work.

Not everybody will be familiar with you as a writer, but your portfolio is a record of achievement and will allow new editors to assess whether they should give you a chance to work for them.

Try to ensure that as many pieces of work that you submit as possible have your byline. This is your name credited to a piece of work, and will effectively become the writing brand that readers will recognise and editors will use to pigeonhole your specialities and abilities.

Writers who have made a name for themselves through specialising include people such as:

- Andrew Davidson: business interviews
- Christian Wolmar: railways and transport
- George Monbiot: environmental issues
- Lynn Barber: celebrity interviews
- Nigel Slater: food
- Quentin Willson: car journalism.

Specialist or generalist?

You may want to decide what areas you will write about. Some writers are specialists who concentrate on just one very specific area, whether it be the mechanics of fish farming, corporate law, or the life and works of sixties singer–songwriters. There is probably a living to be made writing about any of these topics, and hundreds of other niche topics.

Other writers are more generalist, turning their hand to any subject that is thrown their way. The best journalists can become almost expert in a subject they knew nothing about before they received their brief, and forget all they've learned as soon as they get the next commission.

Freelancing in your spare time

It can be easier for writers who already have a job to try their hand at freelancing in their spare time. This can be a good way of assessing whether there is enough work in the market to make it worth your while to go freelance full time. On the other hand, you may see freelancing as a way of making a bit of extra money on the side.

It can be a bit awkward balancing the requirements of a full-time job with the need to hit a freelance deadline, so it is best not to take something on if it will impinge on your full-time job. Remember what is paying the majority of your bills. If, on the other hand, you can make it work for you, then it's a great way of broadening your experience and building up your confidence that you could go freelance full time at some point.

Blogging

Another good way of getting started is through blogging. Although this will almost certainly generate no income to start with, it is an increasingly powerful way of getting your voice heard, especially if you can develop an entertaining and engaging stream of content.

Publishers increasingly monitor blogs as a source of book or even TV ideas. In recent years, books that came directly from blogs include:

- *Belle de Jour*
- *Girl with a One Track Mind*
- *Julie and Julia: A Year of Cooking Dangerously* (which also became a film with Meryl Streep)
- *Shit My Dad Says* (which also became a sitcom)
- *The Joys of Engrish*.

Even if you are not plucked from obscurity for a big bucks publishing deal, blogs are a great way of developing your style and tone of voice. They also give you an opportunity to build an audience of your own by commenting on other sites, suggesting links to your own content and inviting readers to subscribe to RSS feeds or Twitter updates.

Tools of the trade

Being a writer is relatively light on tools. A computer, a notepad and a phone, and you are away. The internet has been a real boon to writers, both in terms of providing new avenues for their work and giving them an invaluable research tool. Pre-internet research could have meant going to local libraries and sifting through books, microfiche or piles of old newspapers and magazines. You might even have had to call people and ask them to post you reports, information and pictures, which would arrive days or weeks later, if they showed up at all.

Now the world of information is at your fingertips, and it has brought a huge boost to productivity. Simply put, you can get more done in a shorter period of time.

> **Startups Tip**
> You need to be aware that not all information online is accurate. Just because something is published does not mean it is correct. Libel is an ever-present danger, so take care with online resources. Always double check the veracity of something if it is going into print.

A room set aside for work is handy, but not essential. Some freelancers work from the kitchen table once the breakfast things are cleared away, or a desk in a bedroom can become their workspace. The important thing is to treat your workspace as a workplace and try to have as few distractions as possible. Don't use your freelance career to catch up on your favourite daytime soap opera.

Qualifications

There are qualifications for writers, but it's not like being a doctor or lawyer – you do not actually need any paper qualifications to ply your trade. Having said that, a writing or journalism course can sharpen up your writing style and prepare you for the world of paid writing. It almost goes without saying that good English is a necessity.

You also have to have an inquisitive nature, confidence to speak to people, and an ability to think on your feet.

There is a world of difference from writing essays for your English literature degree and writing an article that will capture the interest of the passing reader. There are tricks of the trade that you learn from a course, although the best way to improve is simply to keep writing.

Being a writer is a work in progress and there is always something new that you can learn, especially with the growing importance of the internet. Digital media skills are becoming more important for journalists, as is the ability to multitask. A writer may now be asked to supply pictures for a story, so photography skills can be a boon. Video is another format that you could be asked to supply, so the ability to edit or upload video could be useful.

And don't forget the old skills. Shorthand is in some ways a dying art, as people either don't learn it or don't use it, relying on portable recorders to back up their interviews. These are great, but if you record somebody for an hour, it will probably take about three times as long to transcribe the interview. With a shorthand interview, you can be selectively editing as you go along and then transcribe a much shorter interview.

Respected training courses and advice are listed below.

↪ **The National Union of Journalists (NUJ):** offers both new and established journalists advice and information on training, and the courses are designed to help meet the demands of journalism in the digital age. A suite of courses covers multimedia skills – including writing for the web, podcasting, website building and video blogging – on top of traditional skills such as newswriting.
www.nujtraining.org.uk

↪ **The National Council for the Training of Journalists (NCTJ):** the NCTJ is the standard for journalism training. Through its examinations and the courses which carry its accreditation, it equips aspiring journalists to find their first job, and helps working journalists to progress to the next rung up the ladder. The website lists a range of courses including journalism, sub-editing, magazine, broadcast and sports journalism.
www.nctj.com

↪ **PMA Media Group:** introductory and short courses are run by PMA Media Group, a respected editorial trainer with a good track record of helping trainee journalists get their first job or make a start in freelancing.
ww.pma-group.com

↪ **The London College of Communication:** the college has a strong reputation for its journalism courses and has specialised courses

covering various aspects including photojournalism, sports journalism and broadcast.
www.lcc.arts.ac.uk

Where can you get work?

As a writer there are various ways you can get work. Some writers will operate in just one area, where others will straddle different sectors. The important thing when approaching any new source of work is to do your homework and know your audience.

Newspapers and magazines

According to the website Media UK (www.mediauk.com), there are 1,600 newspapers in the UK and almost 2,000 magazines. These are just the ones they list. There are probably others that are obscure enough not to have been noticed. Many of these publications have commissioning budgets and are constantly on the lookout for new ideas and new writers. By being methodical and targeting those publications that you can offer something to, you can start to build a writing career.

Trade magazines

Trade magazines are not necessarily considered the sexy end of the media market – although they do cover such cool areas as fashion, advertising, fast cars and travel. And some of them have become profitable by targeting niche sectors which need to advertise to specific communities of individuals, such as doctors, engineers, lawyers and designers. Consequently, they may have more generous commissioning budgets than some better-known publications. Don't disregard trade titles just because they sometimes have funny names. *Plastics and Rubber Weekly* anybody?

Copywriting

Organisations of all sizes and types need to communicate with various audiences and they need people who are good with words to do that. Often those people aren't within their own organisations and they will go looking elsewhere. Copywriters may be required for marketing materials, catalogues, internal communications or corporate events. It can be a tough market to get into and the work can sometimes be a bit boring, as you need to be able to deliver quite an unswerving corporate line throughout communications, but it is potentially very lucrative.

Contract publishing

Many organisations have their own magazines, which they send to customers. These include supermarket chains and retailers, car manufacturers, drinks producers, airlines, mobile phone companies, banks, utility providers and software companies, to name a few. The object of the magazines is to promote customer loyalty by keeping customers aware of everything the company does and alerting them to new products and services the company can sell to them. Many are produced by specialist media companies called contract publishers, although companies also produce them in-house. Some of the bigger contract publishing companies include:

→ BBC Customer Publishing

→ Cedar

→ Haymarket Network

→ John Brown

→ Redwood.

They are represented by the Association of Publishing Agencies (APA) www.apa.co.uk.

Smaller companies also produce their own publications, usually in-house. Be alert to any opportunity to produce content for them, or even to produce the whole publication for them.

PR agencies

Public relations (PR) companies produce press releases for their clients as well as lots of other written material. This can include reports, case studies, roundtable write ups and biographies. Occasionally they will outsource this work to professional journalists that they know.

Corporate communications

Companies have their own in-house communications teams who handle such tasks as dealing with the media, communicating with their staff, providing information for investors and analysts, and producing other corporate literature. Like most areas of activity, teams have become stretched in recent years and more work is outsourced. Watch out for the possibility of corporate communications work for companies, and let people know that you are available for such work.

Book publishers

Even if you don't have a bestseller in you, there may be opportunities for you in the world of books. Some titles – non-fiction mainly – may commission several writers to cover a particular topic. If you have a specialisation, it can pay to let book editors know that you are available. They may be open to new authors, although as this excerpt from the website of travel publisher Lonely Planet shows, the odds can be stacked against you.

'Each month we receive many applications from people who want to be authors for Lonely Planet. We read them all, then invite those with promise to submit a writing sample. We set the bar high. Last year out of over 500 applications we recruited eight new authors. We have more than 200 skilled and experienced freelance authors working on guidebooks from Sydney to Senegal and currently all our needs are met. If you're interested in being an author for LP, come back to this part of the site (www.lonelyplanet.com) each month for the latest update, and if we're recruiting for someone with your expertise, please drop us a line.'

New publishing models

In the past few years a number of companies have sprung up, offering the chance to write online on specialist subjects. These can be as varied as medical features, entertainment or gardening – basically anything that readers will be interested in. The model recruits writers and requires them to produce a set number of articles a month. These are usually short and sharp pieces produced to a tight deadline. Writers may get a basic monthly fee and extra payment depending on how many people read their articles, or they may be paid purely on the number of clicks they attract.

Writers are unlikely to pay all their bills in this way, but it may be a useful additional revenue stream for specialists who can write quickly and to brief on their subject.

WANT TO KNOW MORE...

Companies that operate this new publishing model include:

- About.com
- eHow.com
- Suite101.com.

Speech writing

This is a very specialist area, but somebody has to write speeches, and it's quite often not the person who delivers it. This can be a branch of corporate communications or it can be part of the entertainment industry. After-dinner speakers, for instance, may use a ghostwriter. But so might a groom at a wedding, who is anxious to impress.

Getting customers in the first place can be tricky, as it is a small market and one that only the wealthy can usually afford. However, you can establish yourself by advertising locally or in club/ association newsletters, or anywhere people might need a speech writer at some point in time, such as wedding planners, event organisers or local start-ups. By building a reputation as a good speech writer, you can start to move up the food chain and charge higher rates.

Eight rules of corporate writing for journalists

By Simon Clarke, freelance writer and lecturer in online journalism at the University for the Creative Arts in Farnham (www.freelanceunbound. com).

In the current climate, some hard-pressed journalists may be thinking they'd like to get out of underpaid, overworked hackery and into the cosy, cushy world of corporate writing.

But freelancers who fancy dipping their toe into the water need to be aware of some cultural differences between corporate communications and journalism that can derail them.

Here, then, are eight key rules for anyone who wants to make the jump from journalistic bear pit to corporate feather bed.

1. **Get used to red tape.** Freelance journalists are used to getting a call or email asking them for a feature and giving them a more-or-less coherent brief. A couple of thousand words later, you send in an invoice and wait for a cheque or BACS payment. (And wait. And wait). Dealing with big corporates is different. My brief stint doing corporate work for a big energy equipment supplier involved getting set up as a supplier, signing a mutual non-disclosure agreement, providing quotes for work to generate purchase orders and filling out a range of financial-type forms. There was also a four-page 'supplier integrity guide' to digest. Many freelancers by their nature seek to avoid this kind of thing and will give up at the first hurdle. Don't. Just bear in mind that, once you're in the system, those freelance payments are a bit more reliable than 'the cheque's in the post'.

2. **Embrace 'reply to all' emails.** It's called corporate *communications* for a reason. Everyone communicates with everyone else all the time. Expect to receive constant email updates, memos and reminders as the project you're working on progresses. Likewise, make sure everything you send to one person is copied in to anyone else remotely relevant. Don't worry about wasting people's time: employees in large companies love this – it proves that they are important and valuable and always in the loop.

3. **Don't think for yourself.** Journalists take pride in being able to interpret a scanty editorial brief and take a feature somewhere interesting off their own bat. Don't be tempted to do this in the corporate world. If any question or uncertainty at all occurs to you, ping out an email to everyone involved (see above) and don't carry on too far with a project without getting a response. Corporates tend to be very clear about what they want from their communications and they want you to deliver it. Exactly.

4. **Keep it plain and simple.** Very plain. Drain all the colour out of your writing. Keep it as straight and factual as possible and avoid colourful turns of phrase and expression. Remember that much corporate output needs to be understood in offices and markets around the world, so its readers are often not native English speakers. In fairness, this does not make your writing bad – in fact, it needs a lot more discipline. Sticking to the facts, writing plain and clear English and assuming your readership is global is actually increasingly relevant advice for online writers generally. But it *is* a bit boring.

5. **Avoid anything controversial.** Even if you've been used to writing very soft features, where no news is bad news and problems are always challenges, it's still difficult to get used to the corporate horror of real language. This applies to everything, especially quotes that sound like a real person has said them. Think you can't write something controversial about a management improvement programme? One interviewee's inflammatory comment that 'people see things that annoy them every day and want to fix them' had to be quickly altered to read: 'Now when people see things that could be improved, they have the tools to do something about it. It's satisfaction for them and a win for the business.' If not a win for engaging writing.

6. **House style matters. A lot.** Newspaper and magazine house style used to matter a lot more than it does now, given the changes in production processes the media is going through. Even in the old days many journalists would be a bit careless about house style, as they relied on sub-editors to get it right. But the corporate style guide is law, and anyone writing for company publications must obey it. In journalism you sneer at companies that try to insist you use ® and ™ symbols on their products. In corporate writing you must follow this guidance slavishly. Be warned.

7. **Learn to love Microsoft Word's 'Track Changes' function.** As a journalist you will probably never have used this – or even be aware of

its existence. But Word's ability to keep visual track of all the changes made to a document by different authors and editors is a godsend in the corporate world. Because, yes, in the end this is editing and approval by committee, and all the committee members must be acknowledged in the process. And when you manage to miss out one of the changes because you can't decipher the chaotic Word document, it's *your* fault.

8. **Most of your time is not spent writing.** Even if you're on an hourly rate, you'll probably have to quote for jobs – and there are many factors affecting how long a corporate job will take. Meetings, email communication, getting up to speed with corporate systems and intranets and learning how to use track changes will all eat time and must be allowed for in your quote. As a rule of thumb, you should double the time you estimate it will take to allow for all the palaver.

If after all this you're still undaunted, think of the upside. While the past two years has been grim for journalism, as newspapers and magazines close and aggregation websites pay £6 an hour for 'churnalism' thrown together by raw graduates, in the corporate world journalistic skills are valued – even prized – and its offices are, in comparison with the newsroom, paved almost literally with gold (well, at £25–£35 an hour basic, it's nearly the same).

It's something at which many journalists might have turned up their nose in better times. But things being what they are, the corporate world can look a great deal more attractive than the publishing house. Get it right and build a good reputation, and the rewards become even higher. Even if you have to wade through in-house jargon to do it.

How to become a freelance web designer

Nearly everyone has a next-door neighbour whose 'genius' 16 year old is a web designer. But it's safe to say, that's not really the level you're at when you start thinking 'web design business'. If you are planning on setting up a web design agency, you need to aim higher than the standard-issue sites born of amateur enthusiasm: web design is a highly competitive area.

The dot-com bubble has long burst, but nowadays, just about every business needs an online presence. At first there was a rush for everyone to have a website, but now the emphasis is on the most innovative and exciting, so brands have to continuously refresh their websites. Whether it's through new design or the latest in interactive content, the current trend for innovation means that web developers and designers really need to keep up to date with the latest technologies and to keep the creative juices flowing in order to beat the competition.

Getting started

The good thing about web design is that it doesn't take very much to start up. You don't need to put more than a few hundred in the pot, as you can happily work from your living room. And you don't need to have a doctorate in online design or advanced programming, either. Perhaps the most important skills and qualifications for starting in web design are a certain amount of know-how, an open mind and a thirst for knowledge.

When starting out, research what the average daily rates are and be firm with how much you charge; it's not uncommon for new designers to charge £500 for a whole website but if it takes two weeks, and you're charging £50 a day, that is really not enough to cover your costs, let alone make a profit.

Tools of the trade

As a freelancer you may work from a client's office or from home. At any rate, you will need a computer that is powerful enough to run the software packages you need. For many designers, this means a Macintosh, but there is no reason why you shouldn't favour a PC.

You will also need an HTML editor, such as Dreamweaver, and a graphics editor such as Photoshop to help with image manipulation. These are the two most common packages, but there are free alternatives such as Kompozer, Amaya and Screem (for Dreamweaver), and GIMP, Krita and Cinepaint (for Photoshop).

As a web designer, it is also pretty near essential that you have a website of your own that showcases what you can do. This should include a list of your services, examples of your work and contact details. This will often be the first contact that a client will have with you, so it has to impress from the start. Take time to create a website that shows your abilities to the fullest. Make sure that your stationery and email signature include the URL.

Qualifications

If you know enough about web design and development to get started you'll probably find that you can learn by doing. If you're IT literate then the 'learn as you go' approach will probably suit you, but it is perhaps a risky way to go if you are entering the tough market of the 2010s. While you don't necessarily need to have several letters after your name, or to be a figure in the industry before starting up, it may make life easier if you are well known – or at least well read – first. It's not a bad idea to work towards this: why not aim to establish a reputation as an expert in your field? That way you can differentiate yourself from the legion already established in the industry.

Nowadays the quality of design work is so high that you have to be really, really good to actually get work. The current trend for innovation means web developers and designers have to keep up to date with the latest technologies in order to gain an edge over the competition. Fine-tuning your expertise and building on your knowledge by reading books, articles and blogs is a key part of developing your freelance career.

Where can you get work?

As with a freelance journalist, web designers have to be constantly alert to work opportunities. Most companies have a web presence of some sort, but competition for this is intense. There are a lot of other designers after the same business.

If possible, start your freelance career by getting some regular work from an existing employer. This will give you a bedrock on which to build and ensure that you don't have to constantly worry about work.

As well as your most recent employer, contact previous companies that you have worked for and let them know that you are available for freelance work. Contacts are everything as a freelancer, so make sure that you spread the word about your freelancer status as widely as possible.

Find out about companies in your local area and make contact with them. They may value having somebody local that they can turn to for their web design needs, especially if you are more competitive than bigger agencies. Make sure that you do good work for them, even if the project is quite small. You never know what mighty oaks may grow from small acorns.

> ## Startups Tip
> When you finish a job to the satisfaction of a client, ask them to refer you to any other clients that may need web work.

As well as looking locally, be aware that the internet means that you can work for people anywhere. Job boards may provide a source of work, but beware of getting involved in a race to the bottom in terms of rates. There will always be someone who can work for less than you, but don't sell yourself short. Decide on a rate that you can accomplish a job for based on its size, complexity, deadline and how much work you have on. Then stick to that rate.

WANT TO KNOW MORE...

Job boards that have web design work include:

- www.peopleperhour.com
- www.technojobs.co.uk
- www.theitjobboard.co.uk.

Web design is a constantly developing area, so make sure that you stay on top of the skills that are most prized; steer your work efforts towards those and away from overly commoditised areas. If you do a job that uses a new skill, make sure that all of your clients know about it, either by emailing then or by writing about in on a blog.

How to become a freelance photographer

Like the world of print, photography has been revolutionised in recent years by digital technology. Now that most of us carry the tools for taking a decent quality picture in our pockets, as well as sending it to a third party or uploading it directly to a website, you might think that the market for old style photography was waning.

However, there is a big difference between a snap grabbed on your mobile phone and an orchestrated shoot or quality image taken at a dynamic event such as a sports match or a press conference. In our visually literate world, clients still require good imagery for a range of things: advertising, press releases, websites, staff newsletters, catalogues and annual reports.

Photography is an interest that can be developed into a freelance career. You can do it full time or part time. Many freelance photographers choose to keep working in a regular job while they build their freelance photography business. By doing this they can build up their portfolio and start to earn some income from their photos before making a decision to quit their job and work full time as a freelance photographer.

Getting started

Anybody can take pictures and get better at taking pictures. The key to developing a career as a photographer is to be able to sell those images, or better still, to work out what images people will pay for before taking them.

Learning the ropes

Traditionally, photographers have worked as studio assistants to learn the ropes. This provides a great background to the craft of the trade and insight into the different types of photography that you might pursue. Some photographers are generalists, doing a bit of everything:

studio portraits, school pictures and corporate work. Others operate as specialists in more narrow fields such as fashion photography, sport and weddings.

Working for a photographer will also provide an insight into the business side of being a photographer. You will be able to see the rates that can be charged for various types of work, the costs involved, and the amount of work you need to do to turn a profit.

If you can't find a local photographer who will take you on, another option is to undertake a quality photography course. There is a wide range of courses available, ranging from evening classes to undergraduate journalism courses that cover the skills of photographic journalism. Work out which one is best for you by speaking to the course tutors and working photographers.

It is never too early to start selling your work. Developing a portfolio of your work is crucial, as this is the main way that potential employers will judge your skill, style and areas of interest. In the early days a portfolio can be as simple as a loose-leaf folder with your best shots in it. Increasingly, clients will want to see something online too, so whether you upload images to a site such as Flickr or invest in developing a bespoke website, don't neglect the web as a marketing opportunity.

First jobs

Start by pitching for freelance commissions from clients who may use imagery. These can include newspapers, magazines, local businesses, theatre groups, associations or news agencies. It may prove tough to get commissioned at first, so try covering newsworthy events and look to sell the pictures to newspapers or magazines afterwards.

In the early days you may have to get used to having a lot of doors slammed in your face, and a lot of rejection. Don't take it personally. Not everyone will need your services, and the more you hone your pitch, the better you will become at working out what is a genuine lead and what is a waste of time. Sometimes 'no' will mean 'not now', and a follow up call in a few months may bring work.

Be confident in your approach and do your homework before picking up the phone.

⇥ Who is the person you should be speaking to?

⇥ What is the company's line of business?

⇥ How can your services help them?

⇥ What will you charge them?

⇥ If they can't speak now, can you follow up in a few days/weeks/ months?

Be methodical in chasing work. Try and develop a system for developing leads. You could check out local ads for companies that may need photography, or you could work your way round advertising agencies or publishers that will commission imagery. Whatever your approach, remember to treat it like an important part of the job. You can only profitably take pictures with a confirmed commission or the realistic likelihood that somebody will buy the shots.

Tools of the trade

Digital technology has slashed the cost of cameras and photography generally. You do not need to purchase ultra-expensive printers or photography equipment to be a freelance photographer.

Having said that, the cost of a professional standard camera, lenses, flashes, stands and reflectors will soon mount up. You will also need more than one camera, for different situations and as a back-up in case one camera fails on the job. If you are looking to do indoor studio portraiture, you will need a studio of some sort, and should consider other items such as softboxes, grid systems, bare bulbs and umbrellas as essential kit.

For indoor studio work, you may also need a supply of props and backdrops. If you plan to photograph babies, you'll need a separate set of props and equipment.

Software such as Adobe Photoshop is the industry standard for work on individual photos, though some photographers work with Lightroom, which is also made by Adobe. You shouldn't rely on software to get good images, but it can be a useful tool to finesse pictures that may have a few gremlins.

Photography is very time sensitive. You may only have a set time slot to get the pictures you need, and if your kit lets you down you are in deep trouble. It is not unknown for photographers to be sued by clients for providing unsatisfactory work. Wedding photographers in particular live in fear of something going wrong on the big day. It can be worth looking at professional indemnity insurance to protect yourself against such claims. Of course, your expensive kit should also be well insured – no camera equals no job.

Another important tool for a photographer is a vehicle of some sort. It's not impossible to carry your kit around with you, but being mobile means you can get to shoots quicker, and on to the next piece of business. Unlike writing, where you can interview over the phone or even email, photography calls on you to be in a set place at a set time. If you don't make it, you've lost the job. It's better to be in control of your own destiny when it comes to travel than rely on public transport.

Qualifications

As stated earlier, you can either work your way up the ladder as a photographer's assistant or take a course. There is no need to do either, but both options will endow you with experience and a working method that you would otherwise have to develop yourself by trial and error.

There are plenty of photography courses available in the UK, and many of them also include some element of business studies to ensure that students achieve a level of commercial sense. In this respect, it is probably better to aim for a photography degree, rather than a fine art degree with a photography option. The best courses are taught by practising photographers, and the newer universities are more flexible in allowing them to continue to practise professionally rather than requiring that they be research-active academics.

Colleges that run photography courses include the following.

→ The London College of Communication offers a BA in Photography that includes direct access to the experience of talented hands-on photography tutors. The course encourages you to generate visual ideas and teaches the techniques to put them into practice (www.lcc.arts.ac.uk).

⇥ The University of Westminster offers a number of specialist photography degrees including BSc Clinical Photography, BSc Photography and Digital Imaging, BA Contemporary Media Practice, and BA Photographic Arts (www.wmin.ac.uk).

⇥ The University of Wales, Newport offers specialist BAs in documentary photography, which has an emphasis on photojournalism. It also has a BA in Photography in Fashion and Advertising (www.newport.ac.uk).

⇥ The University of Bedfordshire offers a Digital Photography and Video Art BA Hons course (www.beds.ac.uk).

Experience is a crucial determinant of success in photography and people will pay more for somebody who has a longer track record. Somebody with 20 years of experience and good work will beat you to jobs unless you give clients a reason to go with you. Price competitively, but don't start out too low. If you give someone very cheap prints now, and they come back later for more, they'll expect the same deal.

When it comes to building your portfolio, make sure that it represents a range of good work. The temptation will always be to include your absolute best photos. However, if your work for a client doesn't equal those, then they'll be disappointed. So, when you're hunting for clients, show good work that you can reasonably expect to duplicate in terms of quality and talent.

A note on copyright

Under UK law, the person who takes a photograph is the first owner of the copyright in it – unless you are a staff photographer, in which case the employer owns it. This also applies to commissioned photographs as covered in the Copyright, Designs and Patents Act 1988.

Only the copyright owner can license the copying of a photograph. That means reproducing the work in any material form, which includes storing the work in any medium by electronic means. In cases where a client wishes to use a photograph, an appropriate licence must be granted and fee paid.

Where can you get work?

Newspapers

Local newspapers are the proving ground of many photographers. The round of fetes and council meetings may not get the pulse racing, but they will build your experience and show that you can get the shot required. It may also help you to break into the nationals, although competition is fierce. Both national and local newspapers use freelance photographers as sources of images for their publications.

Magazines

There are thousands of magazines in the UK with image requirements. These vary from news-style shots of events that are of interest to their readers, to studio-based products shots or portraits. Because of their frequency, magazine imagery is often more planned, so there is an opportunity to study their requirements and present your portfolio to the creative director or picture editor. *The Freelance Photographer's Market Handbook* is a useful guide to possible clients. You can buy it from the Bureau of Freelance Photographers' website (www.thebfp. com).

Image libraries

Many organisations buy so called 'stock shots' from image libraries. These are providers of often generic or conceptual images that can be used to illustrate anything from magazine layouts to advertising campaigns.

The pictures are supplied by individual photographers and marketed by the image banks. They will negotiate a fee for an image dependent on its usage. For example, the fee will be higher if it is seen by a large audience, or if it is used in a place of particular prominence, such as on a product's packaging. The upside is that you are more likely to get your images in front of a large number of buyers. The downside is that you lose control of the selling process and the agency can take a large fee.

However, image libraries are a great way of deriving additional revenue from pictures that you have already taken, and a good image may be used again and again, providing income each time.

Different libraries may have different specialities. Here are some examples.

- Alamy is the world's largest independent stock photo site (www. alamy.com).

- The British Association of Picture Libraries and Agencies (BAPLA) has a search facility (www.bapla.org.uk).

- Mira is a stock agency of the Creative Eye cooperative (www.mira. com).

- Photolibrary.com is an independent producer and distributor of stock photography.

- Rex Features is a photographic press agency and picture library specialising in celebrity, feature and entertainment markets (www. rexfeatures.com).

- Stockshot.co.uk is an adventure sports library.

- The Wellcome Trust is the leading source of images on medicine and biomedical science (http://medphoto.wellcome.ac.uk).

Book publishers

The market for illustrated books is expanding, and although publishers rely heavily on picture libraries for images, there is scope for photographers who can deliver material on specific subjects at a specific time. Specialist areas such as wildlife and food photography are good examples of this. Getting on the radar of publishers is the hard part, and there is no substitute for networking and perseverance here. Introduce yourself and try to keep a dialogue going with someone who commissions photography.

A related area is cards, calendars and posters. Although it can be similarly tough to break into, the rewards are worthwhile.

Advertising and marketing

Brands and their agencies need imagery for their campaigns, catalogues and communications. As well as the blue-chip brands that will probably use well-established advertising specialists, there is a whole raft of activity that probably has lower budgets but still requires bespoke imagery. Getting in contact with marketing departments or ad agencies can give you access to this work and may lead on to bigger and better things.

Corporate work

Businesses may need photography for a host of reasons: for press purposes, internal communications such as house magazines, trade communications, marketing, or simply to have a nice picture of the chairman. Stay alert to opportunities to work directly with companies.

Weddings and portraits

Weddings and portraiture are still strong markets as well as specialist markets that you can build a career around. Both require a certain level of experience, however, and are probably not to be entered into as a first step on the freelance ladder. Look to serve an apprenticeship with an established and respected photographer to learn the ropes before branching out on your own.

Useful links

- Editorial Photographers UK and Ireland: www.epuk.org
- Master Photographers Association: www.thempa.com
- The Association of Photographers: http://home.the-aop.org
- The Royal Photographic Society: www.rps.org
- The Society of Wedding and Portrait Photographers & The British Professional Photographers Associates: www.swpp.co.uk

How to become a freelance tutor

Tutors can provide additional or sole teaching across a range of academic and non-academic areas. If you have a recognised expertise in a particular discipline, and the ability to impart knowledge to others, tutoring can be a valid career option. It can also be a useful supplementary income for newly qualified teachers and graduates, supply teachers or retired teachers.

More and more parents are looking to supplement the teaching their children receive in areas such as maths, English and science. Educational think tank the Sutton Trust estimates that a quarter of schoolchildren nationally, and 43% of children in London, receive private tuition at some point in their lives.

It's not just academic teaching that is sought. Individuals may want private instruction in any number of areas, from playing a musical instrument to learning a language. The internet has also made online tutoring more achievable, so tutors do not even have to be in the same place as their charges.

Getting started

The first step in developing a private tuition business is to establish whether there is a market for your skills. You may find that people approach you and ask whether you can provide tuition, in which case the answer is obviously yes. If you are not sure, do some research by looking at small ads in local newspapers where tutors may advertise their services. You could also check out noticeboards in the local library, newsagents or shopping centre. Speak to parents you know and ask if they use tutors and what they think of the service they receive.

Next you need to find out what the going rate is. Ring up local tutors and ask what they charge. The website www.hometutorsdirectory. co.uk provides a guide to what tutors charge in various parts of the country and for various subjects.

This will give you an idea of what you can charge. Remember that rates will vary according to several factors.

- Location: some areas will bear higher rates, particularly London and the South East.
- Your experience and qualifications.
- Where the service is provided: do you need to factor in travel expenses, or other costs if tutoring in your own home?

-> Will you have to provide any materials?

-> Will you tutor to single pupils or several at one time? One to one tuition will carry a higher rate.

It makes sense to start with a small number of clients and develop your business from there. This gives you an opportunity to hone your skills and to ensure that you are offering a quality service. If it seems as if you are sacrificing quality to quantity, business will soon drop off. Word of mouth is very important in the tutoring sector, so the best thing you can do to develop your business is to ensure that those first customers want to tell their friends about how good you are.

Outside of recommendation, keep your eyes open for new ways to promote your services. Some local authorities maintain lists of private tutors – find out if yours does and send it your details. There are also a number of tuition agencies, both national and local, which are a useful way of picking up a few new pupils. These will charge commission on work they put your way. They are also a good way to market your services, because they check the tutoring credentials of prospective tutors. Parents who contact them requiring tuition are reassured that only those people who are well qualified are accepted as tutors.

Tools of the trade

Your experience and qualifications are your main requirements as a tutor, unless you are providing tuition in a subject that requires specific equipment. In these instances, it is important that the tools you use – be it a piano, computer or lathe – are up to scratch. Don't scrimp on buying these items, as they will reflect on your tuition as much as your knowledge and expertise do.

Similarly, clients will expect you to be abreast of developments in your specialist subject, so make sure that you keep your knowledge up to date by undertaking ongoing training, subscribing to relevant subject journals and reading and using the most up-to-date study materials. Where tuition is for exams such as GCSEs and A levels, it is essential that you stay up to date on curriculum developments.

It is useful to keep a record of all lessons on a record sheet, listing the lesson number, date, main topics covered, exam questions completed and homework set. These will help you to produce progress reports for your clients. It is also useful to be able to refer back to what you have done in previous lessons, as well as conveying a professional image to pupils and parents.

The other main decision for any tutor is where they will carry out tuition. If you go to pupils' homes, you will have to factor in additional costs for travel and time between appointments. Working from home is a better use of time, but you will have to present a professional image with a smart and well-appointed study where tuition will take place.

Qualifications

Currently in the UK there are no minimum or maximum qualifications that private tutors require to offer a private tutoring service. However, a minimum requirement sought by most tutoring agencies is a foundation degree or HND if you wish to provide tuition for academic subjects.

Most private tutors have a degree or equivalent. Some have a Postgraduate Certificate in Education (PGCE), but you do not require one. It will qualify you to teach in schools and colleges, however.

As important as your paper qualifications are your demeanour, teaching style and presentation. Tutoring is a very personal undertaking and clients have to be happy that you can provide them with the service they require. Factors in developing a successful freelance career include:

- → adaptability: every student learns at a different rate and in a different way. There is no one size fits all approach, so be flexible

- → communication skills

- → enthusiasm: people learn more effectively from tutors who have a genuine love for their subject combined with an ability to pass on their knowledge

- → organisation: you will be working for a variety of clients, and that can be a lot of plates to spin. But to the client, it must all appear seamless

- → subject understanding.

Where can you get work?

Parents of schoolchildren studying for exams, or simply in need of an extra bit of support in specific disciplines, are the largest part of the private tuition market. Tutors can also pick up work from college students and private individuals who simply want to improve their learning in certain areas.

Online tutoring is a growing area. Both the trainer and participants use their computers to meet online, rather than meeting face to face. The online learning environment is dynamic and may require the use of a headset, a webcam or the aid of some other technology in order to communicate over the internet. Successful online training requires that you take some time to understand how different technologies such as VOIP or web conferencing can be used.

WANT TO KNOW MORE...

More information on web tutoring can be found at www.onlinetutoringworld.com.

Agencies and directories of tutors can be a way of attracting more business. Agencies will charge commission for any work that they put your way and directories may have a listing fee. There are many companies offering this service, including:

- www.capitaeducation.co.uk
- www.firsttutors.co.uk
- www.hometutors.org.uk
- www.hometutorsdirectory.co.uk
- www.localtutor.co.uk
- www.personal-tutors.co.uk.

CRB checks

Criminal Records Bureau (CRB) checks have to be carried out by law by some employers, particularly for those working unsupervised with children and vulnerable adults, who undergo an enhanced check. However, private tutors do not have to be vetted.

It will cost you to have an enhanced disclosure check, but if you tutor mainly young children it could pay for itself in providing parents with some peace of mind. Individuals can't apply directly to the CRB to have themselves checked. Your application has to be endorsed by a registered body such as a school or tuition agency. Some registered bodies, called CRB umbrella bodies, will endorse applications of private individuals. An umbrella body is a CRB Registered Body that allows smaller, non-registered employers to use CRB checks. They act as an intermediary between you and the CRB, offering experience that helps move the process along quickly.

More information is available from www.crb.homeoffice.gov.uk.

How to become a freelance graphic designer

We live in a visual age, and the look and feel of everything we see has been created by a designer. While some designers work in-house for companies, there are many businesses that only have an intermittent need for design skills. Those companies will often turn to freelance designers for those needs.

A freelance designer can design and tweak logos, create and amend websites, produce publications and marketing materials, or even design products. Some of these jobs, such as computer games design, are specialisms, but graphic work may be produced by a generalist who has an ability to handle a broad range of design briefs.

Getting started

Like many freelancers, designers often start working for a business with design at the heart of what they do, such as publishing companies, advertising agencies or design consultancies. These companies recruit design graduates and help develop their careers. However, after working in-house for a while, they may decide that a freelance career suits them.

Working as a design freelancer can entail either working in a client's office or undertaking projects from home. If you are opting for the latter route then you will need to consider the costs of kitting yourself out to do the work. As an employee, your company provides the high spec computers and software packages that are necessary. Buying this yourself can involve a hefty upfront investment.

If you already have the equipment to freelance from home, you can gauge whether or not freelancing will suit you by taking on some extra work while still in a job. Like many forms of freelancing, designers may find that their old employer is their best source of work initially – find out if there is any work that you can take with you when you go freelance.

Put together a portfolio of your work to give potential employers an idea of your ability and style. Set up your own website to showcase the best of your talents. In the case of a freelance graphic designer, a website is effectively your business card.

Familiarise yourself with as many graphics programs as you can. Photoshop, QuarkXPress, InDesign and Illustrator are standard, but other programs may also be valuable if you are dealing with animation, Flash or video.

Designers often work as part of a team, so identify likely partners you could work with. In the early days especially, it is unlikely that you will get well-paying jobs directly from clients. Clients often have elaborate pitch processes that are geared towards getting the best price and service from their suppliers. It is unlikely that as a one-man band you will be invited on to a pitch list. However, by working with an agency that supplies a complete communications solution, you can get some of the business.

Make a list of all likely agencies in your area that may need designers and contact them with a view to arranging a meeting where you can show them your portfolio and discuss what you can do for them.

Tools of the trade

As mentioned above, as a freelancer you will have to invest heavily in the design tools that your market is using. Before you do invest what could add up to several thousand pounds, speak to designers and agencies to find out what they recommend using, what is absolutely essential, and what is simply nice to have. Computer design equipment is costly, so you only want to buy what you need to do your job.

For starters, you will need a computer which is powerful enough to run the software you will be using. Programs such as Photoshop, Dreamweaver and InDesign place heavy demands on your machine. Make sure that you invest in something that is up to the job. A slow machine will slow the pace at which you can work and will only serve to frustrate you in your efforts.

As well as a good computer, a large display screen with good resolution is also important to allow you to see what you are producing. A good quality printer is also useful for printing out drafts. It is unlikely that you will be able to justify the cost of a top of the range printer, and at any rate you can use a bureau for best quality prints that may be needed for a presentation. However, a lower specification printer is handy.

Software requirements will depend on the type of design you are involved in, but could include:

⇥ back-up and restore software

⇥ coding software

⇥ FTP client

⇥ graphics software, such as Photoshop, Illustrator and InDesign

⇥ virus protection.

Workspace is also important. Design is a sedentary activity, so ensure that you have an area that is comfortable to work in, with a desk and chair that feel good to you. It is easy to neglect this aspect of your job, but as you spend a third or more of your day in one space, it should be comfortable.

Qualifications

According to the British Design Council, two-thirds of the people working in the sector hold at least a level 4 qualification, which is roughly equivalent to a certificate of higher education, while half have qualifications higher than level 4 (Higher National Diplomas, foundation degrees, degrees and above).

Many graphic designers have an art school or design degree background, but often what employers are looking for is a great creative eye and a familiarity with the kinds of tools they use. Whether you achieved these skills at college or on the job is almost immaterial. Likewise, as a freelancer, most of your clients will be more interested in your portfolio of work than your degree grade.

Having said that, design is a dynamic area where ongoing training is important, both in new software packages and techniques, and in the sort of business skills that freelancers of every stripe will find essential. Developing your skills in pitching for business, time management and client liaison can all help develop your business.

Where can you get work?

Previous contacts are a great way of establishing yourself as a freelancer. The design world can be very incestuous, so being networked with other designers can lead to referrals and job offers. Often designers will not be available when a piece of work comes their way, and the client will ask if they know anybody else who could take it on. Make sure that you swap details with other designers when you encounter them so you can reciprocate if you are ever in a position to turn down work.

Make a list of all the companies and agencies in your area that might have a design requirement. Cold calling is never fun, but it is a discipline that you will need to develop, especially when times are tough. Make contact with local firms, charities, marketing and PR agencies and try to stay in contact. They may have no work at present, but circumstances change and persistence pays off.

Job boards are an increasingly common way for clients to solicit invitations to bid for work. Opinions vary as to how valuable this can be for gaining work. Because it often doesn't matter where a designer is based, you could find yourself pitching against somebody from a market with much lower costs, which can make it impossible to pick up a decent rate for a job.

However, it is worth keeping an eye on job boards. Many are very US centric, so if you want to find out about UK specific jobs, look for ones that are based in the UK. Here are some to check out.

→ **Brand Republic:** for jobs in marketing and marketing services, the site allows filtering by sector, discipline, pay level, location, and salary (www.brandrepublic.com).

→ **Freelance Students:** positions across a range of industries and disciplines for freelancers (www.freelancestudents.co.uk).

→ **Guardian Jobs:** an advanced search function allows you to specify terms among thousands of up-to-date jobs listed (www.guardian.co.uk).

→ **Job Rapido:** all kinds of work are featured on this general site, including many freelance openings (www.jobrapido.co.uk).

→ **People Per Hour:** a bidding site catering for a range of jobs that can be carried out remotely (www.peopleperhour.com).

You can also sign up with specialist recruitment agencies that may be able to put work your way. This can be useful in the early days when you are developing your contacts. However, bear in mind that they will charge a commission, so the sooner you can find your own work the better.

> ## More information on design
>
> - British Design Innovation (BDI): www.britishdesigninnovation.org
> - Chartered Society of Designers (CSD): www.csd.org.uk
> - Design Council: www.designcouncil.org.uk
> - National Design Academy: www.nda.ac.uk
> - Royal Institute of British Architects (RIBA): www.architecture.com
> - The British Institute of Interior Design (BIID): www.biid.org.uk
> - The Directory of Design Consultants: www.designdirectory.co.uk

How to become a freelance consultant

The title 'consultant' sounds more high powered than mere freelancer, but the reality is that anyone can become one, providing they have a skill that is in demand from other businesses. When you become a consultant, you offer skills, knowledge and expertise that businesses or other people can use.

A consultant gives advice, solves problems, makes recommendations, or provides specialist work. This may be knowledge that a client company doesn't have in-house, or it may be that an organisation can't see the wood for the trees and wants somebody else to come in and offer them a new perspective on their business.

A consultant is usually paid by the hour, day or project, on commission, or based on performance. They are independent contractors and not employees of the hiring organisation.

Consultants can work in many areas such as human resources, finance, marketing, IT, recruitment, logistics, civil engineering or design. Basically any dedicated area of knowledge that can be used for the benefit of an individual or organisation can provide the basis for a consulting career.

Getting started

There are lots of jokes about consultants, such as:

Q. How many consultants does it take to screw in a light bulb?

A. How many can you afford?

However, starting a consulting career is not something to be undertaken in a light-hearted manner. The first thing you need to do is discover what you can consult about. What knowledge and experience are you able to impart to clients? Do you have a specific area of expertise, or are you something of a generalist? If the answer is the latter, then you may not be able to tell clients anything they don't already know. Although some people would joke that telling people what they already know is exactly what many consultants actually do, your aim should be to shine a light on people's problems and point them towards the right solution for them. You must know everything there is to know about your sector so you can share this information with your clients and improve their business.

Using your sector expertise and knowledge, try to work out where there is potential for business development. Are there particular areas where businesses you know have need of your skills?

Develop a business plan and pitch that explains what value you can add to an organisation by getting involved with them. For instance, if a small company does not have a marketing or PR function, offer to develop their strategy in this area by working for them one day a week or a few days a month. By identifying a specific business challenge and presenting a solution, you can kickstart your consulting career.

When you start your consulting business, no one will know who you are. Learning how to network is essential to getting work. The essence of much consulting work is that you are providing solutions for problems that businesses may not even realise they have, or that they only have a dim recognition of.

Network with other businesses and prospective clients to find out about the firms in your area and to build up your business. As well as business associations, networking organisations, community groups and local chambers of commerce, social groups such as the local golf club or gym are excellent opportunities to meet potential clients.

Word-of-mouth is the best form of advertising, so spread the word about what you are doing and what you can offer. Work your contacts book, including former employers, work colleagues, and college friends. These people can tell others, who pass on the word in turn, until you start getting calls from prospective clients.

Remember to ask for client testimonials or referrals to offer to potential clients. By being given the opportunity of speaking to, or hearing from, satisfied customers, new clients are more likely to use you.

Networking sites such as LinkedIn form an invaluable new way of building up your network. Create a compelling profile which succinctly and forcefully explains what you do and your experience, and point people towards it as an online CV. Try to get clients and former work colleagues to 'recommend' you online, as this will boost interest from potential clients.

When you are starting out as a consultant, it can be a good idea to find a mentor who can show you the ropes. Even if you are an expert in your own field, there is a lot to learn about the skill of successful consulting, and somebody who has already been there and got the T-shirt can fast forward you through the early stages and help you avoid common mistakes.

Tools of the trade

You will need an office to work out of, and to store details of your ongoing consulting projects. Organise your office so it's set up for your consulting business. You will need to set up secure files for all of your clients with information specific to them, as well as keep files dedicated to your business for tax purposes.

It is important to keep track of the hours you work and to charge clients accordingly. It will be useful to develop a set of terms and conditions that will detail your working methods and what clients can expect from you.

A clear paper trail on projects is important. Here are some of the documents that could be useful.

- → Action plan: a breakdown of what has been agreed in a meeting as key action points and who is responsible for them.

- → Briefing form: the key questions to ask concerning a project.

- → Client record form: an internal document recording what you need to remember about the client, such as who's who, first impressions of the business, personalities of main players etc.

- → Invoice: for billing the client.

- → Timesheet: recording the hours you put into a project.

Sites such as www.simply-docs.co.uk carry template documents that you can download and amend to your requirements. However, for peace of mind you may want to speak to your own lawyer to help draft documents that are watertight for your own needs.

You should also evaluate your need for professional liability insurance, which will protect you if a client files a suit regarding how you did or didn't fulfil your obligations. This coverage may be necessary, in addition to any general liability policy you may have, to protect you in the event that clients sue, claiming that you caused them financial loss or interruption of services.

As a freelancer, you don't have the financial resources of a big company to back you up in the event of a lawsuit. Some companies require independent consultants to carry liability insurance when working on a project for them. You can assess your risk based on the type of work you do, the clients you take, and how well your contracts shield you from this type of lawsuit.

Qualifications

As stated before, anybody can have a business card printed up with the title 'consultant' on it. However, depending on your area of consultancy, there may be sector specific qualifications that are either essential or that make you stand out from the crowd.

Find out what qualifications and industry body memberships existing consultants in your sector have, and what they actually mean. A string of letters after your name may look impressive, but if they are nothing more than a flaky correspondence course, they may well fool no one. Conversely, if you do have a genuinely hard to achieve qualification, flag it up in your presentations and pitches, explaining what it means and why it helps you deliver a better service for a client.

Consulting is all about knowledge transfer, so learn about new topics related to your specialty in order to increase your clientele. Keep up to date with new business consulting trends and attend courses and seminars.

There is also general business consulting training that you can undertake, which will help you to improve your consultancy technique and develop your career.

The Institute of Consulting (www.iconsulting.org.uk) offers a range of recognised qualifications for the business consulting profession that are awarded by the Chartered Management Institute. If you are looking to move into the profession, gain independent validation of your skills or consolidate and embed your existing skills whilst networking with your peers, its programmes are delivered by a range of training providers.

Where can you get work?

Businesses, governments and non-profit agencies use consultants because they need specialised skills or knowledge. In most cases, they hire consultants because they only need the skills or knowledge for a short period of time or for less than a full-time basis.

Like most freelancing, consultancy is a word of mouth business, so it is important to work your contacts book. Make sure that contacts know that you are now carrying out consultancy work and ask them to spread the word.

Check out relevant job boards for your sector and register your details with directories of consultants and industry associations, which often maintain their own lists of active consultants.

However, bear in mind that the more proactive you are, the more business you will build. Treat every meeting as a business opportunity, and prepare an elevator pitch that briefly explains what you do and how you can help businesses. Ensure that you carry business cards with you at all times and collect the details of potential clients. More importantly, make sure you follow up on initial contacts to stay front of mind with them.

 Checklist

- ☑ Research which freelance career will be right for you.

- ☑ Look to get experience in your chosen area before you decide to freelance full time.

- ☑ Decide whether you will have a specialisation or whether you will be a generalist.

- ☑ Make sure you are properly equipped to do the job.

- ☑ Find out the different sources of work that you can pursue. Try to think laterally and not simply stick to the obvious ones.

- ☑ Look to pitch ideas to get new clients.

- ☑ Assess whether you need any special qualifications or training.

↪ *CHAPTER 3*

Setting up as a freelancer

📖 What's in this chapter?

Now that you've made the decision to become a freelancer, you need to start planning how to achieve it. There are certain things you need to do in order to tie up loose ends with your existing employer as well as creating the correct framework for your new job.

In this chapter we'll cover:

→ how to resign

→ registering as self-employed

→ business structures you can follow

→ rules and regulations you'll need to be aware of.

Leaving employment

It may seem as if this part of the going freelance equation is the simplest. Having decided to opt for self-employed status, you simply pack your bags, flip your boss the bird and bid your colleagues a fond 'See you, suckers!' farewell.

Of course, it's not as simple as that. For one thing, your old employer is probably one of your best sources of future work in the short and long term. Unless you have absolutely loathed working for your old boss, don't burn any bridges. Even if you have disliked the job intensely, it's worth swallowing hard and reviewing your options.

For one thing, working for a company freelance is different from being on the payroll. You will be divorced from all of the office politics. It will hopefully be just one job among many, and you may find that as a freelancer, you are looked on slightly differently than as a member of staff.

Planning to leave

For all of these reasons, it's best to leave work on the best possible terms and to do it properly. Give proper notice that you are leaving, and seek to explain your reasons to your boss and colleagues. It won't paint you in a very positive light if you slap down your letter of resignation and tell them you are heading for the door in the shortest possible time.

If you can, and if the company asks you, try to be flexible on your leaving date. They may find it difficult to replace you, which is flattering in its own right, and also gives you a chance to create a lasting legacy at the business. It may be tempting to spend the last month (or however long your notice period is), taking it easy and boring your colleagues silly with tales of your new life. That approach won't get you far in the long term, and certainly won't create much goodwill when you are looking for work from them in future. You may also need to go back to your old employer at some point for a reference, either for a project you are undertaking as a freelancer, or should you decide that you want to get another job.

Look to be as helpful as you can, both in terms of setting a leaving date and preparing for your departure. Putting together a job description for your successor will help whoever takes over from you. Make sure you pass it on to your line manager and their boss, as it will also underline how much you did at the company and what a hard act you will be to follow. Offer to sit down with the new person and take them through what you did.

Similarly, if there is an offer of an exit interview, take the opportunity to be constructive about the organisation rather than simply slating it. Again, there could be an opportunity to suggest ways that they could do things better, and pitch for elements of your job that you could take with you. Prepare a business case for this in advance and follow it up.

It's best to resign in writing, even though a verbal resignation is perfectly legally acceptable. However, putting things in writing gives you a chance to put your thoughts together coherently, rather than simply blurting out the first thing that comes into your head. You can also make it clear how much notice you are giving and when your last day will be. You may also want to add any reasons as to why you are leaving.

Template resignation letters

If you are stuck for words about how to resign, use a template letter from a website such as:

www.i-resign.com/uk/letters/letters.asp

or

www.thecvstore.net/blog/sample-resignation-letters/

Notice periods

An employee who has worked for a company continuously for one month or more must give notice of their intention to leave. The notice period should be included in a written statement of employment which must be issued within two months of starting work.

Notice could be anything from a week to several months, often depending on how valuable you are to the company.

The minimum statutory notice period which must be given by an employee is at least one week's notice if employed continuously for one month or more by that employer. This minimum is unaffected by longer service. This minimum notice does not apply to independent contractors or freelance agents.

Unless a contract states otherwise, notice can be given on any day. The notice period runs from the start of the day after the day on which notice was given. So if a week's notice is given on a Monday, the period of notice will begin on the Tuesday and expire at the end of the following Monday.

Some contracts of employment contain special terms about notice: for example, in contracts of employees who have access to information that you wish to protect from a competitor. In this case you may be asked to go on 'gardening leave' whereby you will serve out your notice period outside of the office, normally due to confidentiality issues.

If you do end up having to spend time on gardening leave, you will not be able to undertake any freelance work during this period. It is very important that you check the details in your contract and understand what you can and cannot do during this period. If you break the terms of your contract during gardening leave, things could get messy and your employer could try and refuse your notice pay and benefits.

> **Startups Tip**
> More advice on resigning can be found at: www.direct.gov.uk/
> en/Employment/RedundancyAndLeavingYourJob/DG_10026688.

Pay and benefits

If you are leaving your job then you should be entitled to pay and benefits during your notice period.

Your benefits if you resign

If you have voluntarily quit without good reason, your local Jobcentre Plus can delay your Jobseeker's Allowance. If you are claiming constructive dismissal (where your employer's behaviour has forced you to resign), make sure the centre knows. If you can't claim Jobseeker's Allowance, you may still be able to claim a hardship payment, which is a reduced amount of Jobseeker's Allowance.

The Citizens Advice Bureau website provides further detail on benefits entitlements: visit www.adviceguide.org.uk.

Pension schemes

If you have a personal pension plan, you can take it with you if you change jobs. If you were paying into a company scheme, you should be able to get a statement of the current value of your pension fund. You may be able to transfer this to another scheme, or into a personal pension plan.

Being paid for holidays you haven't taken

Full-time employees receive a minimum of 5.6 weeks (28 days) paid holiday every year. However, some employers may provide additional holidays as part of your contract. When you leave your job, you should be paid for any unused legal minimum holiday allowance, although your contract may say that you lose untaken contractual holidays. If you have taken more leave than you have earned, your employer can't normally take the money from your final pay unless it has been agreed beforehand. Check your contract for details.

Getting your P45

When you stop working for an employer, they will normally give you a P45 form. This is a record of your pay and the tax that's been taken from it so far in the tax year. You will need a P45 form to give to your new employer. As a freelancer you will be responsible for your own tax returns; however, your P45 is an important document as it records your PAYE contributions when you were employed, and these will need to be included on your tax return. Chapter 7 looks at filing your tax return in more detail.

How do you know if you are classed as a freelancer?

It may seem a silly question, but freelancers work for other companies and the nature of the relationship may not always count as being self-employed.

Business Link recommends that if you are not sure whether your work counts as self-employment, you should ask yourself the following questions.

- Do you present your clients with invoices for the work that you do for them?
- Do you carry out work for a number of clients?
- Are you responsible for the losses of your business as well as taking the profits?
- Can you hire other people on your own terms to do the work that you have taken on?
- Do you have control over what work has to be done, how the work has to be done and the time and place where the work has to be done?
- Have you invested your own money in your business or partnership?
- Do you provide any major items of equipment which are a fundamental requirement of the work you carry out?
- Do you have to correct unsatisfactory work in your own time and at your own expense?

If you can answer 'yes' to most of these questions, then you are probably self-employed already, and should let HMRC know this immediately if you have not already done so. You may be fined £100 if you fail to register within three months of becoming self-employed. There is no fee for registration.

Registering as self-employed

Setting up as a sole trader, or freelancer, is by far the easiest and quickest way to start a business. A sole trader is the simplest form of business where one person owns and runs the business.

Before you start

Pretty much anyone can set up as a sole trader, although there are certain types of work that require obtaining a licence or permit from your local authority, such as child minding, taxi driving or street trading.

If you're planning on running your business from home, you may have to pay business rates for the part of your home that you use for business purposes, depending on whether or not you use that part for domestic purposes as well. For example, if you work from a computer in your bedroom it is unlikely you'll have to pay business rates, but if you work from a separate office, this may entail paying business rates.

Another thing to bear in mind if you're working from home is whether or not you need planning permission. If you propose to make any changes to your house for business purposes, such as building an extension, or if you're likely to cause disturbance to your neighbours, it will probably be necessary to get planning permission. Contact the planning department of your local authority for more details.

How to register

Anyone who becomes self-employed must register for income tax and National Insurance contributions with HM Revenue & Customs (HMRC). This can be done either online, by phone or by post. However, it is far quicker and more convenient to sign up online. When registering you will need to provide your National Insurance number – if you don't have one, contact Jobcentre Plus.

While it is not possible to register in advance, it is important that you inform HMRC as soon as you start working. Upon registration, you'll need to provide the following information:

- name
- address
- National Insurance number
- date of birth

--> telephone number

--> email address

--> the nature of your business

--> start date of self-employment

--> business address

--> business telephone number

--> if relevant, the full name and date of birth of any business partners.

Self-assessment

As a self-employed sole trader, you'll have to complete a self-assessment tax return for HMRC. This involves filling in a tax return form, either online or in paper, in which you inform HMRC of your income and capital gains, or in which you may claim tax allowances or reliefs. We'll look further at filling in your self-assessment tax return in Chapter 7.

Registering for VAT

If you expect to have a turnover of more than £77,000 a year, VAT is applied to your earnings, which also involves contacting HMRC. To register for VAT you'll need to fill in one or more forms, depending on your business' circumstances, and then submit them to HMRC.

To apply for basic UK VAT registration, download and complete the form VAT 1 from HMRC. You can also voluntarily register for VAT even if turnover is below the £77,000 threshold. This has certain benefits, such as portraying the business as being bigger than it is and allowing you to charge and reclaim VAT.

Maintaining records

It is important that you set up a financial record-keeping system, which includes maintaining all records that show your business income and expenses. For more information on the type of records you'll need to keep, see Chapter 7.

National Insurance contributions

If you're self-employed you must pay Class 2 and Class 4 National Insurance contributions. See Chapter 7 for details on what you'll need to pay.

All this may appear quite daunting at first, but if managed properly it's really not as overwhelming as it seems. The best thing you can do is stay organised, maintain your paperwork, and flag up any tax or self-assessment deadlines in your diary well in advance so you have adequate time to prepare for them. We'll cover all of your new admin responsibilities in Chapter 7.

Business structures and understanding IR35

Some freelancers choose to structure their employment affairs in a more tax efficient manner by setting up limited companies, or umbrella companies, in order to keep more of their earnings and pay less tax.

The different business structures

A limited company is a way of setting up and business that limits your liability if things go wrong with your business. As a sole trader your personal assets are potentially at risk. As a limited company you should be able to keep more of your income. An umbrella company is a company that acts as an employer for agency contractors allowing them to claim more on expenses.

This is entirely legal, if done properly. However, HMRC pays close attention to the use of such instruments and is always on the look out for 'disguised employment' where individuals are effectively employees of a company, but don't pay the corresponding income tax and National Insurance contributions a permanent worker would.

What is IR35?

IR35 is a piece of tax legislation that was introduced in 2000 to counter tax avoidance by contractors and freelancers. It aims to tackle the practice of taking income from a limited company through large dividends and small salaries which were used to provide tax benefits. The tax rules apply to certain employed and self-employed individuals.

Details of the intermediaries legislation, as it is known, were given in a 1999 Budget press release numbered IR35, hence the usual reference. The aim of the legislation is to eliminate the avoidance of tax and NICs through the use of intermediaries, such as personal service companies or partnerships, in circumstances where an individual worker would otherwise:

⇢ for tax purposes, be regarded as an employee of the client; and

⇢ for NICs purposes, be regarded as employed in employed earner's employment by the client.

IR35 has made headlines since its introduction and has also left a lot of people mystified.

The statement sought to clamp down on one-person services companies where individuals ostensibly acted as employees of a company, but avoided PAYE by charging for their services under a contract. The practice was particularly common among IT contractors.

Under the rules, HMRC states that a contractual worker falls under IR35 if:

⇢ he or she works for a client but does not invoice the client directly for work carried out, but instead:

⇢ the client contracts an intermediary company, which then effectively employs the worker. It is easier for the client – if dissatisfied – to dispense with the services of the intermediary than it would be if it employed the worker directly. The client also avoids PAYE, National Insurance or tax issues.

<ul>
<li>→ the intermediary company, in which the worker has at least a 5% beneficiary interest, then invoices the client for the worker's efforts.</li>
<li>→ the worker takes their earnings in the form of a dividend (a distribution of net profits of the company to its shareholders) on which NICs aren't paid.</li>
</ul>

Hence, the HMRC argues, the worker is effectively employed, but in tax terms is self-employed and is therefore a 'disguised employee'.

A tricky issue

The problem that has arisen is that contractors UK-wide are arguing the HMRC's cloudy definition of the difference between self-employed and employed workers makes IR35 too arbitrary. As such they want more balanced assessments of what constitutes a 'disguised employee'.

The reason this is important is because the IR35 regulations only apply to situations where the worker would be deemed to be an employee of the client, if it were not for the presence of the intermediary.

Guidelines exist where, at first glance, it would be easy to assume the contractor fell under IR35. For example, a contractor can work for a single client for good business reasons without being employed solely by them, and the length of the contract in itself is not a factor in determining whether the contractor is caught in IR35.

And if you do fail IR35, the HMRC is obliged to provide an explanation as to why it related to your circumstances.

Where the worker is deemed an employee, all earnings of the intermediary company (which effectively becomes an employee itself) become subject to PAYE and National Insurance. In cases where companies have believed themselves outside IR35, this can mean hefty back payments.

On 6 April 2007, Chapter 9 ITEPA 2003, also known as Managed Service Company (MSC) Legislation, was introduced. MSC Legislation applies to individuals providing their services through intermediaries which meet the definition of a Managed Service Company, and an intermediary must consider whether MSC Legislation is applicable to them before considering IR35.

Intermediaries that do not meet the definition of an MSC must continue to consider IR35. If you think you may fall within the scope of IR35, it's important to seek immediate professional advice from your accountant. Official guidance can be found on the HMRC website: www.hmrc.gov.uk/ir35.

Latest developments

The Office of Tax Simplification has been taking a long hard look at the overall tax system, including IR35. Its interim report on small business tax simplification is unclear about what the future may hold. On the one hand it calls for greater enforcement of IR35, but also moots its abolition. A third option is to do nothing, so an issue which has created much head scratching and argument since its introduction seems no nearer being resolved at the moment.

The report can be downloaded at www.hm-treasury.gov.uk/d/ots_ small_business_interim_report.pdf.

Are you IR35 compliant?

Freelancers or contractors need to ensure that their contracts and working practices show that they are outside HMRC's tax rules.

IR35 rules apply to individual contracts, so you need to be vigilant that each contract is compliant, as you could be caught out on one and not another. For this reason, it may be worth having new contracts reviewed by employment experts to ensure they are watertight. HMRC can backdate tax liabilities if you are found to be inside IR35, so it is vitally important that you avoid common pitfalls.

What constitutes compliance can seem vague, but there are certain areas that HMRC will look at in determining your IR35 status. Some may be more important than others, such as substitution, control and the mutuality of obligation, but the taxman will look at the overall picture in deciding each case.

If you are only contracting for a short period, it may make more sense to fall inside IR35, thus avoiding the work and expense of alternative arrangements.

Substitution

As the contract is not between your client and you personally, you must be able to provide a substitute in the event that you cannot work. The right to substitution must always be a genuine one, with any costs of providing the substitute met by your own company. If your client does not agree to this, or if a substitution clause does not appear in your contract, you are likely to fail IR35.

Control

Your contract and working practices should indicate that you do not perform your duties in a manner akin to a normal employee. Freelancers and contractors are entitled to work when and where they see fit. As long as you complete the work you are paid to do, you are free to decide how and where you do that work. If your client sets your hours, you will fail IR35. Freelancers and contractors typically work free from a great deal of supervision.

Mutuality of obligation

Is the client obliged to offer you work, as an employer would an employee? Similarly, are you obliged to take on work after the expiration of your contract? A service company will expect to sign a contract to provide a fixed amount of work, invoice the client, and get paid for it. Continuous work from the client is another strong indicator of employment.

Equipment

Employees are generally provided with equipment by their employer, but a self-employed freelancer or contractor would expect to provide their own equipment. This could include a computer or machinery.

Payment

Although a regular payment cycle is seen as an indicator of employment, experts see it as being inconclusive, and HMRC's

Schedule E manual states that a self-employed person can also be paid by the hour/day, etc.

Financial risk

The self-employed may risk their own funds when working on a project. This could mean payment for training, equipment, running costs, and materials. Financial risk could also take the form of quoting a price for a contract, with the consequent risk of bearing the additional costs if the job overruns.

Employee benefits

Are you entitled to employee benefits? This need not be as significant as a pension; it might include use of the company canteen, for example. If yes, then the contract may be subject to IR35. After some time on a project, some freelancers and contractors may feel as if they are gradually becoming 'part and parcel' of their client's organisation. To sidestep this suggestion, skip meetings which don't relate to your contract work: avoid using staff facilities such as the canteen or gym, and being managed by permanent staff or managing them.

Other factors

Some potential indicators of self-employment include professional indemnity insurance cover, company stationery, a company website and VAT registration.

Previous freelancers and contractors

Has HMRC judged that a previous freelancer or contractor performing the same work has fallen inside IR35? Ask the client about this in advance of signing the contract.

Rules and regulations

As a freelancer, you are effectively a small business, and you are subject to many of the same laws that any small business is. This is all stuff that you will probably never have had to deal with before, but you can't afford to bury your head in the sand.

Health and safety regulations

As well as tax issues, freelancers may be caught up in various health and safety regulations involved in working from home. Obviously it will depend on what your business is. A freelance mechanic working out of the garage at the side of their house will have to comply with the same level of red tape that any other garage would. Similarly, if you want to install an industrial oven in your garden to further your dream of being an artisan baker, you will need to consider any potential planning issues.

If you are planning to set up and run a 'work at home' business, there are a number of points to check before you begin. Working from home can affect your mortgage, your home insurance, your tax situation and even your neighbours.

Depending on the nature of your business, it is a good idea to check with some of the following:

-> your mortgage lender or landlord/freeholder: information about using your home to run a business may be contained in your mortgage or tenancy agreement

-> your insurance provider, to see if you need to take out extra insurance

-> the Valuation Office Agency (VOA), to see if you will be charged business rates

-> the Health & Safety Executive (HSE) or your local authority, to find out the health and safety aspects of running a work at home business and how to do a risk assessment

-> your neighbours, to make sure they have no objection to you running your business from home

-> the planning department of your local authority, to see if you need to make structural changes to your home

-> if running your business from home means that the use of the building changes a lot, or the activities that you undertake have an effect on the area where you live, you may need to apply for planning permission from your local authority.

The Health and Safety at Work Act

The Health and Safety at Work Act 1974 places duties on employers, employees and the self-employed to protect health, safety and welfare. Generally, everyone involved in work in any capacity must take proper care for themselves and other people. If you are self-employed, you will have to do some of the things that are done for employees by their employer, such as assessing the risks of your work.

This might seem like a lot of red tape, but it is a good discipline to ensure that your workplace is as safe as possible, even if it is primarily your home.

If you use your home as your business workplace, you must carry out a health and safety risk assessment to identify any possible hazards to yourself, workers, visitors and other members of your household. See pp 90–93 for more on health and safety risk assessment.

Copyright and libel

Other areas you will need to be aware of are things like ensuring that you are running legal software on your computer. It may be tempting to run off a copy from a friend, but the consequences in terms of fines will make a dent in your cashflow, as well as your liberty. You can face up to 10 years in prison and unlimited fines for infringing software copyright.

For writers, the issue of libel is one that needs to be taken seriously. Although most litigants will go after a publisher in pursuing an action, there are increasing instances where individual writers are sued, even though they may have little money. Libel cover is available, although it is no substitute for being aware of the law in this field. Ensure that your knowledge is up to date and retain a copy of *McNae's Essential Law for Journalists* on your desktop.

Currently, the government is looking at the whole area of libel in the UK with the aim of ensuring that laws do not crush debate or freedom of speech. However, for now the current legal framework applies.

Data Protection Act

Another legal area to be aware of is the Data Protection Act 1998. If you obtain, store or use personal details from customers, suppliers or other contacts, it is a legal requirement that you comply with the principles of the Data Protection Act.

These include the requirements that information must be fairly and lawfully processed; used for specified purposes only; accurate and up to date; kept secure; and not transferred outside of the European Economic Area without adequate protection.

 ## Checklist

- ☑ Make a proper plan to leave work: this includes checking your contract carefully with regards to your notice period.

- ☑ Let your employer know that you are leaving in writing, giving a firm leaving date.

- ☑ Don't burn your bridges: you never know when you may work with former employers or colleagues again.

- ☑ Register as self-employed within three months of going freelance.

- ☑ Decide what set-up is right for you – self-employed, limited company, partnership, umbrella company – and take appropriate advice on how to structure your business

- ☑ Think like a business from the start.

- ☑ Ensure you are aware of any rules and regulations that will affect your new business venture.

↪ **CHAPTER 4**
The home office

📖 What's in this chapter?

For many freelancers, working from home can be part of the deal. Establishing and kitting out a proper workspace is essential to becoming a productive homeworker. This chapter will help you to shape your new workplace, including:

→ creating the right environment
→ equipment you will need
→ setting up a home office
→ technologies to help freelancers
→ finding a work-life balance.

Working at home

Most freelancers will work from home at least part of the time. It's part of the joy of going freelance, after all – swapping the daily trudge to a distant place of work for a swift commute from bed to desk.

But to make your home function as a place of work, you need to be serious about establishing where you will locate yourself in your home, and what sort of kit you need. After all, you will be spending the best part of every working day in this space, so you should make sure that it is comfortable and conducive to doing good work.

I am typing this while looking out over my garden. An apple tree is showing a decent crop of Bramleys for this autumn, and an array of garden birds pecking at the feeder regularly have me grasping for the birdwatcher's guide on my desk.

However, I am conscious of the fact that this is where I'm supposed to work, so I've tried to keep it free of distractions. There is no TV (although the internet now serves practically the same diverting purpose), the traffic is a distant muffle at the front of the house, and the same can usually be said for my children.

As much as possible, I've tried to make my workspace somewhere that gives me no excuse not to be productive. Any failings in that area have to be down to me.

Creating the right environment

Modern technology means we are no longer office bound. Freelance businesses can be run from a spare bedroom, the attic, or even a garden shed.

The idea of being chained to your desk from 9 to 5, sandwiched between a lengthy commute, may seem like your only option, but improvements in technology have made working from home not only possible, but often easier than working in the office. High-speed broadband, BlackBerry mobile phones and PDAs have all made working remotely possible, and there's no reason why working from home should have a negative impact on your ability to be successful.

The home front

Working from home generally does mean a better working environment for you, with no distractions such as office politics; at home there's only one person to make tea for. Working from home is also a way of limiting your start-up costs, as you won't need to rent office space.

However, work and home life can never be separated totally, and this is even more exaggerated for those who work from home. The emotional side of working from home should not be underestimated.

Without the buzz of the office, and the ever present sense that the boss could be looking over your shoulder at any minute, self-motivation can be a problem, especially if it's a sunny day and your deadlines seem comfortably distant. Why shouldn't you take advantage of the weather and chill for a bit?

The key thing is to treat your workspace as a workplace, and the best way to do that is to create the right working environment. For some people, it is perfectly possible to work in the busiest room in the house and to crack on with all manner of tasks with the TV playing in the background, kids running riot and the family pet demanding to be fed.

For most of us mere mortals, however, such a set-up would be hell and would have a dramatic effect on our productivity. One of the great things about moving out of an office workplace to your own office is that you get rid of a whole set of distractions: gossiping work colleagues, fielding unimportant phone calls, Dave from accounts dropping by to seek sponsorship for his marathon run, or any number of other things that are part and parcel of everyday life in an office.

Why replace these distractions with a whole new set?

By working from home, you are opting to try to make better use of your time. The lack of a daily commute can free up a couple of hours a day in some cases, so you are ahead of the game already. Don't fritter that time away. Remember what you are trying to achieve by going freelance:

→ greater earning power

→ more time for your outside work interests

→ less stress

→ a better quality of life.

Whatever the motivation for going freelance, it will only be fulfilled if you take working from home seriously.

Thinking about what you want

It's your workplace, so you can afford to make it your own. There's no office services manager saying that you can have any colour as long as it's beige, and if you want to have a calming goldfish bowl sharing your desk, there's no one to stop you.

Having thought about what your ideal home office would be like, the next trick is to marry those thoughts to reality. For most of us, this means the choice between squeezing into a corner of the dining room or possibly using a spare bedroom. In which case, the trendy fireman's pole access is probably out.

Sharing space

A separate workspace is vital. Fitting into a corner of a room may work if you are single. But most partners, and definitely any children, will invade your space constantly if you try to share living space.

Consulting your partner is the key to making it all work. They must be happy to sacrifice the space. Remember that they could be under huge pressure in their own work and may not want to be reminded of the office when they get home. Finding your computer buzzing away in the corner might not be the best way to relax.

Equally, if you are to lose the spare room, discuss the implications. Will you have to keep a bed in the room for visitors, or could you manage with a sofa bed pushed to the back and rolled out on odd occasions?

If you are likely to have regular business visitors, working in a corner of the sitting room is not an option. It is not very professional to have to clear away last night's Chinese takeaway to create a space for them to sit down. You probably won't want to take them upstairs to a spare bedroom either.

Some people are lucky enough to have a house with a ready-made study that is big enough to suit their needs. Others may have an outside room that has already been converted. But others will be starting from scratch.

Here are a few tips to keep in mind.

- Remember that you will be inside this space from 9 to 5 Monday to Friday and possibly longer.

- Try and give yourself a good view. It has been shown that natural daylight has a beneficial effect on productivity. Most professional meetings spaces now make a virtue of rooms with a view outside.

- Make sure the room is well lit, and is warm in winter and cool in summer.

- Try to make a space in a room where you can shut the door behind you at the end of the working day. Separating work and home life is important; otherwise, you may find yourself drifting between the two, which is unfair on both. Although it is sometimes necessary to work longer hours, try to focus on achieving your goals during your normal working hours, especially if you have family who expect to spend time with you.

- Give yourself more room than you think you actually need: you will be surprised how quickly you can fill any given space.

With these points in mind, you need to decide whether to adapt an existing room or whether you are looking at converting the garage or shed outside.

If you take up an existing room, consider other members of your family. Will they be happy to lose that space? If it has an impact on them, are they happy to keep out of the way while you are working and not interfere with the papers on your desk when you are not there?

If you are converting an outside space, check to see if you need planning permission. Also check the building costs and the time required for the conversion. Adding utilities such as lights, water and telephone lines can prove very costly if it is an entirely new installation.

Depending on how near the office is to your home, you may need dedicated telephone lines and internet access. Alternatively, you may be able to access the wireless internet connection, and a wireless phone handset may be within range of the base station in your home.

Again, plan ahead and try to envisage what your requirements might be in the future. Forward thinking can save a lot of unnecessary hassle later on.

Equipment you will need

What you need for your office will depend on your business, but it is a good idea to be as self-contained as possible in your workspace. There is nothing more disruptive to the day than to find that you don't have something to hand and to have to venture into the wider house to find it. Before you know it, you'll by diverted by something: making a cup of tea, switching the TV on, waving to a neighbour and wandering outside for a natter, or a passing Jehovah's Witness noticing that there is somebody at home in the middle of the day.

Sit down and make a list of everything you could possibly need in your workspace. This could include:

- binding equipment
- blinds for the window to prevent glare
- CD player/iPod docking station
- chair
- desk

- desk tidy
- external disk drive for back-ups
- extra chairs or desk for visitors or additional workers on a project
- fan for summer
- files

- → filing cabinet
- → heater for winter
- → kettle
- → laminator
- → lamp
- → PC or laptop
- → phone and answerphone
- → pinboard
- → printer
- → radio
- → scanner
- → shelving
- → shredder
- → stationery
- → storage boxes
- → TV
- → waste paper bin
- → whiteboard.

Not all of these items will be necessary for everybody, and some people will need additional items. Once you have made your list, you can then prioritise the items that you really need to get your job done and look at how you will fit them into your workspace.

How much will it cost?

Not sure what you can afford? Read on to find out how much each option could cost.

Once you have thought about what you want from your workspace, do your sums and look at what you can afford. Bear in mind what is *essential* and what is *nice to have*. Also, consider what specification you need and whether you need to buy everything new. Some items, such as office furniture, can be picked up second-hand from specialist stores for a decent price. This could enable you to get a better piece of furniture for your office dollar than if you simply went down to the local flat pack superstore.

To give you an idea of what you may have to invest, here are a range of basic, mid-priced and expensive alternatives.

In a spare corner

If you're restricted to a spare corner somewhere in the house, you may not have enough space for a full desk.

A more practical solution will be a large work-centre. These usually combine a small desk area with space for a PC, monitor, printer, and filing drawers — all in one unit. You can get also corner workstations that are specifically designed to slot in the corner of a room.

As far as seating goes, you want something that won't get in the way — particularly if this doubles as a corner of your living room.

TABLE 1: Set-up costs for a basic workspace

What you need	Cost
Workstation	£140
Chair	£100
PC and printer	£500 and £70
Telephone/answerphone	£30
Desk lamp	£25
Stationery	£20
Estimated cost	**£885**

Taken from www.startups.co.uk/how-much-will-it-cost.html

Mid-range small office

If you are lucky enough to have a spare room that isn't being used, then you will have more options for your office. Depending on the space available, you may have room for a desk and two chairs, filing cabinet, table and all the essential equipment.

TABLE 2: Set-up costs for a mid-range small office

What you need	Cost
Desk with drawers	£150
Filing cabinet (three-drawer)	£100
Chair (executive)	£150
Chair (guest)	£50
PC and printer	£850 and £200
Telephone/answerphone	£30
Lamp	£25
Stationery	£20
Estimated cost	**£1,575**

Taken from www.startups.co.uk/how-much-will-it-cost.html

Deluxe home office

This really is living the high life in terms of home offices. Unfortunately this is not for those who are counting the pennies. The overall cost of a conversion will be high. If you are really unlucky you could find yourself shelling out for a new staircase, steelwork to strengthen the floor,

TABLE 3: Set-up costs for a deluxe home office

What you need	Cost
Attic conversion	Starting from £17,500
Large desk	£160
Drawer unit	£120
Filing cabinet (three-drawer)	£100
Chair (executive)	£150
Two extra chairs	£100
PC and printer	£1,000 and £300
Copier/answerphone/scanner	£370
Lamp	£25
Stationery	£20
Estimated cost	**£19,845**

Taken from www.startups.co.uk/how-much-will-it-cost.html

installing two velux windows, insulating and plastering the walls as well as wiring up the electrics. That's without carpet and decorations. Installation of a second telephone line can be free of charge with BT if you take out a broadband and calls package, or a triple play package with TV.

If you can manage the costs, though, the set-up includes a large desk with a drawer unit and an executive chair. In case you are holding meetings, you will also have room for two guest chairs and a large filing cabinet.

Buying a computer

Selecting the right machine for your business can be a confusing affair. There is a vast array of choice, which seems to bamboozle all but the most technically minded. The market is becoming even more complex as the computing sector now covers desktop PCs, laptops, PDAs, notebooks, smartphones and tablet computers like the iPad, all of which may use varying operating systems.

The first questions to consider are:

→ what will you use it for?

→ how much processing power the computer will need?

→ do you need a mobile computer?

From there, you can look at some of the options.

Desktop PCs

If you don't need to be out and about with your machine, a standard desktop PC is for you. A PC or Mac should have enough memory and storage to manage most of your needs. A desktop PC is also a bit more robust than a laptop and you can opt for a large screen if your business is graphics based.

Desktop computers are relatively inexpensive and easy to upgrade. However, they can be a bit bulky and take up a lot of space, although newer versions are more slimline.

PCs purchased online or direct from the manufacturer tend to be built to order, which gives the option to select peripherals to suit your budget and needs. You could opt for ergonomic keyboards and large screens, or wireless mice and keyboards if you need desk flexibility.

Laptops

Desktop replacement laptops can match the performance of a desktop PC, but without the bulk and lack of mobility. If you anticipate being on the move a lot, or simply want something that you can put away at the end of the day, a laptop could be for you. They are also useful if you find yourself being shunted from one workspace to another in your house.

Take a good look at the weight of the machine if you anticipate carrying it around a lot. A laptop which seems light and portable can quickly start to feel like a lump of lead if you have to hump it around all day.

Costs for laptops are usually slightly higher than desktop PCs for comparable performance.

Netbooks

These are basically small PCs with limited processing power. They are great for accessing email or appointment lists on the move, or viewing websites, but are not suitable for intensive applications such as working on spreadsheets.

Tablets

Touch-screen operated tablets are, essentially, notebook PCs without a physical keyboard that offer various levels of functionality. They are lighter than a laptop and easy to use and can have as much processing power as a desktop. They allow wireless access to the internet when working remotely.

Although prices are coming down, tablets are still quite expensive and have relatively small screens. Because they are designed to be carried around, they can be more prone to being damaged unless you acquire a protective cover, particularly for the screen.

Computer buying checklist

What to look for when buying the following:

- **Processor:** the faster the processor, the quicker and more efficiently the PC will run. For everyday requirements, a processing speed of around 2.5GHz is ideal for desktop PCs, 2GHz for laptops. If you are downloading large amounts of data or using graphics programs, you may need to upgrade to something faster.
- **Memory and hard drive:** the higher the RAM (random access memory), the more efficiently the computer's operating system will run. You should seek a machine with at least 2GB for business use. Additional RAM can be added at a later date. Look for a hard drive of at least 500GB. Bear in mind that it is harder to add memory to a laptop, so ensure that you buy a machine that has sufficient memory.
- **Monitor:** a larger screen allows you to work more efficiently, and is essential in some areas, such as design. For a very large monitor, a special graphics card may be required.
- **Connectivity:** computers include a selection of standard ports for peripheral connection. USB ports connect printers, keyboards, memory sticks and other peripherals. An ethernet socket enables connection to a network router for internet access. Most laptop computers now have wireless network capability, but a desktop PC may require additional hardware.
- **Operating system:** this controls the functioning of your computer. Microsoft Windows remains the most widely available system, although others include Mac OS X and Linux. Windows 7 is the latest version installed on many machines as the Home Premium edition. You can upgrade to Windows 7 Professional if you think you need it, for security or for running old applications that are based on Windows XP.

- **Warranty and support:** find out what level of support you can get. Some retailers will offer a complete replacement service for a computer that fails. Others offer telephone support initially, with a back-to-base or on-site repair service only in extreme circumstances. It is critical to check the small print. Buying an extended warranty can be worth it as a lack of computer could stop your freelance career in its tracks.

Setting up the home office

Now you've got your desk and chair, laptop and desk tidy, you can start setting things up. Take time to work out the best set-up for you. Remember that you will be spending the best part of every working day in here, so it is important that it is comfortable, safe and stimulating.

If you were in an office, health and safety rules would determine much about the space in which you would be working. Try to apply the following to your own space.

→ **Give yourself room.** It is amazing how quickly you can fill a space up and it is equally amazing how difficult things become once the office is untidy. Projects can get completely buried in piles of paper and you can waste hours digging out that vital note.

→ **Think about the equipment that you will need.** Health and safety officers enforce strict rules about electric cables running across office floors for a reason – you don't want to break a leg by tripping over the wire to your computer.

→ **Consider the mechanics.** Check that there are adequate power points for the computer, printer, telephone and all the other equipment that you will need. Also, check that you have adequate telephone lines. It is easier to have a second line dedicated to the business than to risk your toddler answering the call from your top, but very sensitive, client.

→ **Allow for plenty of light.** Working from home can often mean much longer hours at your desk and often at odd hours of the day and night, so adequate light is essential. Good daylight is also important. It can be very lonely working from home and at least seeing the seasons change can help.

Ergonomics

The HSE, in its leaflet 'Understanding ergonomics at work' states that 'Ergonomics aims to make sure that tasks, equipment, information and the environment suit each worker.' Poor posture, lack of proper equipment and improper computer set-up can cause stress on certain parts of the body. The ideal ergonomic set-up of a work station is different for everyone, but there are a few simple rules to bear in mind. You should establish a comfortable working position that enables you to avoid stiffness and pain. Do not position the monitor above your head and don't lean forward into the screen.

You can get a workstation assessment by a professional, or you can set up your own workstation by bearing in mind these guiding principles.

- **Chair:** make sure you are using a chair that is adjustable and adjust the height of the chair so your feet can rest completely on the floor. Choose a chair with armrests. Use a footrest if you have one, but don't keep your feet in one position. Position your hips so that they are slightly higher than your knees. Change position by moving your feet, lifting your arms and adjusting your hips throughout the day.

- **Keyboard:** position the keyboard in the centre of your desk with the mouse immediately to the side.

- **Lighting:** the office should be moderately bright.

- **Monitor:** minimise glare by placing it at a right angle to lights or windows. Try to keep the monitor about 20 inches (51cm) away.

Health and safety risk assessment

It may seem a bit over the top to be affected by health and safety legislation when you work from home, but it is your place of work and, as we saw in Chapter 3, the Health and Safety at Work Act 1974 places duties on employers, employees and homeworkers to protect health, safety and welfare.

Most of the literature on the subject of health and safety at work relates to factories, offices, shops and other workplaces. As a freelancer, you are responsible for assessing your own workplace and carrying out work safely.

WANT TO KNOW MORE...

The HSE produces a useful guide to risk assessment for homeworkers.

www.hse.gov.uk/pubns/indg163.pdf.

Some organisations, such as the BBC, publish their own health and safety briefings for freelancers working on their behalf.

www.bbc.co.uk/supplying/freelancers/docs/safety-hs_for_freelancers_v4-1.pdf.

The HSE advises that there are five steps that you need to take to make sure that a proper risk assessment is done. As a freelancer, you can look at these and, with a bit of common sense, adapt them to suit your needs.

Step 1: identify any hazards

Look at what may cause harm to you or anyone else as a result of the work being done in the home. Small hazards should not be ignored as they may result in harm, for example keeping potentially harmful substances out of children's reach.

Step 2: decide who might be harmed and how

Look at who may be affected by the work done at home and how they may be affected; this may include you or members of the household, including children or visitors.

Step 3: assess the risks and take appropriate action

If you come across a hazard that may be a risk to you or anyone's health or safety in the home, you need to decide what steps must be taken to eliminate or reduce those risks as far as possible. What needs to be done depends on whether the hazard is low risk or high risk.

You can determine this by looking at what type of harm or injury may arise and how often it may happen. For example, there is greater risk of an accident from loose trailing wires if there are children in the home.

In the case of loose wires from work equipment, they should be tucked away under a desk or table, or secured neatly out of the way.

Step 4: record the findings

Employers who have five or more employees are required by law to record the significant findings from a risk assessment. This should not affect a freelancer.

Step 5: check the risks from time to time and take steps if needed

It is important to check the risk assessment from time to time, especially if there is a change in working procedures. The assessment needs to take into account any new hazards that may cause harm to your health or safety.

Possible hazards include:

→ excessive noise or vibration

→ fire

→ handling loads

→ hazardous substances and materials

→ psychological hazards, such as stress or loneliness

→ slips, trips and falls

→ using work equipment at home, including electrical appliances

→ your workstation set-up.

You need to evaluate whether a hazard is significant and, if it is, whether you have taken enough precautions to make the risk as low as you reasonably can. You don't have to write down the results of your health and safety risk assessment unless you employ five or more people.

WANT TO KNOW MORE...

More information is available from the HSE website: www.hse.gov.uk.

Technologies that help freelancers

As a freelancer, you have cut your ties with the various functions of the company that help you do your job. For now on, it's just you – you're a one-man band. Thankfully technology is developing at a fast rate to make things easier for those of us who work on our own. From project management to connectivity, and admin to marketing, there are plenty of tools that can help you do your job, and do it better. Here are just a few of them.

Email

Email is so ubiquitous now that it is hard to think what all the fuss is about, unless you can remember the pre-electronic mail age. Rather than being at the mercy of the 'snail mail' service, you can now request information from somebody and receive it in the click of a mouse. Similarly, you can send out information, invoices or begging letters to your contacts instantly. And now, with smartphones, you can access email on the move. The implications of such connectivity on your productivity are huge. It allows you to keep the plates spinning while you are out and about, making best use of downtime.

Choose a service that allows you to download your email to any email program such as Microsoft Outlook, Windows Mail or Mac OS X Mail. Also look to see what the capacity of the inbox is. Some services, such as Gmail, offer unlimited online storage.

Other factors you might want to consider are the amount of advertising that gets thrown at you by the service, its level of spam protection, search facilities, and how it allows you to index files.

> **?**
>
> **WANT TO KNOW MORE...**
>
> Free email services include:
>
> - www.fastmail.fm
> - www.gmail.com
> - www.hotmail.com
> - www.yahoo.com.

Voicemail

With no one to take messages for you, voicemail is another essential tool to ensure that you don't miss out on important calls. Nobody wants to miss out on a commission because they were taking another call or were indisposed. Most land and mobile services have a voicemail service. These may be free, or charge a fee depending on functionality. For example, you may get a free basic service, but have to pay for a service that allows you to leave a tailored message, so people know who they have got through to.

Having your own voicemail message creates a more professional image for your freelance business and makes it more likely that people will leave you a message, which allows you to decide quickly how important it is to return a call. Some mobile services charge for retrieval of voicemail.

If you are working away from your landline a lot, you may want to look for a service that allows remote access to voicemail.

Smartphones

The latest generation of internet phones opens up a whole array of functionality to freelancers. As well as keeping you in touch with the world of work through voice and email communications, smartphones are effectively mini computers that provide a whole lot more. From search facilities, to maps for directions, to location based services that let everyone know where you are, the number and utility of apps that can help freelancers is growing all the time.

When looking to buy a smartphone, consider what your primary needs will be. If email is important, a BlackBerry device may be the better option as email deliverability is more immediate and it offers easier desktop syncing. However, the distinctions between the three main choices – BlackBerry, iPhone or Android powered phone – are increasingly slim.

Cost is obviously a consideration, so shop around for the provider offering the best overall package.

Apps

There are hundreds of apps that are useful to freelancers, and new ones are being developed all the time. Here are just a few that are worth trying.

⇥ **Evernote:** Evernote makes it easy to remember things big and small from your notable life using your computer, phone, and the web. Type a text note. Clip a web page. Snap a photo. Grab a screenshot. Evernote will keep it all safe. Everything you capture is automatically processed, indexed, and made searchable. If you like, you can add tags or organise notes into different notebooks (www.evernote.com).

⇥ **Freshbooks:** an online time management and invoicing system that allows you to stay on top of the work that you do for a clients (www.freshbooks.com).

⇥ **Gwabbit:** an Add-in for Microsoft Outlook and BlackBerry that finds, grabs and adds contacts from your emails to your Outlook address book with a single mouse click (www.gwabbit.com).

⇥ **Gmote:** turns Android into a remote control for a computer, allowing users to run movies and music at a distance. It supports all of the standard remote control features such as play, pause, rewind, volume controls etc. It also has a built-in file browser that lets you select what to play (www.gmote.org).

⇥ **Scan2pdfmobile:** this software uses your mobile phone to scan documents and convert them to PDF files. It all happens on your phone, allowing you to scan documents anywhere – as long as you have your phone (www.burrotech.com/scan2pdfmobile).

FTP sites

Sending large files via email can be troublesome. It can take a long time to send data and large files may not get through a recipient's firewall. FTP sites allow you to upload files to a site and notify the recipient that there is a file that they can download. It's quicker than posting a disk or a memory stick, and there are plenty of free options out there. In line with most free services, functions may be limited, with more premium services only available if you pay for them.

WANT TO KNOW MORE...

Here are some file sharing services to try:

- www.attachmore.com
- www.sharefile.com
- www.wetransfer.com
- www.yousendit.com.

Social media

Marketing yourself and making yourself known to potential clients is an important part of being a freelancer. With the advent of social media sites such as Facebook, Twitter, YouTube and LinkedIn, freelancers can have an online presence without going to the expense of having their own website designed and built. Social media can build awareness of you and your work and provide useful channels to communicate with potential clients and peers. You can also use social media to promote yourself as an expert in your field by contributing commentary and thoughts to cyberspace. In addition, you can use the media to search for partners, to undertake research for projects and to seek advice from a wider group. The important thing to remember with social media is that you will get more out of it if you remain active. It is hard to dip in and out and retain much credibility with other users. Think what you want to achieve through social media and develop your personal strategy around that.

See pp 126–134 for more information on the main social media sites and how to use them to grow your business.

Blogs

Like social media, blogs are a great way of building up your profile by writing and curating information about your area of expertise. Allied with social media, such as Twitter and Facebook, you can become a one-man publisher. The most popular blogging platforms are Wordpress and Blogger, which are both free and offer a range of tools. Other options include Posterous and Tumblr for more visual blogs.

Dongles

When it is not possible to find a wi-fi hotspot, a broadband dongle enables you to keep accessing the internet. These can be bought and paid for on a pay-as-you-go basis, or you can take out a monthly contract if you think you will be using it a lot. Prices vary, as does the amount of material you can download, so shop around.

Online accounting/invoicing services

Staying on top of your paperwork is one of the most important parts of being a freelancer, but it can easily be pushed to the background until you suddenly find yourself overwhelmed by it. Online accounting services work by using software which logs your income and outgoings and produces professional looking invoices. The service can also make filing your accounts at the end of the year easier, and will give you a view of the health of your freelance business.

WANT TO KNOW MORE...

Try these online accounting services:

■ www.clearbooks.co.uk

■ www.crunch.co.uk

■ www.freeagentcentral.com.

Remote PC access

If your work takes you away from home on a regular basis, you can still access the files on your main PC with a remote access service. This allows you to remotely control your desktop, transfer files between computers, print remote files, share a large file without using email, FTP, or a third-party site, and share your desktop with another person. You have to leave your computer on and connected to the internet. The service can usually be trialled for free and is then charged on a monthly or annual basis.

WANT TO KNOW MORE...

Try these remote access services:

■ www.gotomypc.com

■ www.logmein.com

■ www.webex.com

■ www.yousendit.com.

Skype

Skype and other voice over internet protocol (VOIP) services allow you to slash your phone bills, particularly if you call overseas often. Users have to download Skype software to their computer and can then call other Skype users for free as a phone or video call. It also has an instant messaging service that allows you to chat and send files. You can also make calls to landlines or mobiles at cheap rates by buying Skype credit or taking out a subscription. For virtual teams working at one remove, the service makes video conferencing relatively simple and cost-effective.

Cloud storage

Backing up your computer files is essential if you don't want to lose work and invoices. You can use external hard drives and memory sticks, but another option is cloud storage. This is where your files are stored on a remote server, giving you access to them wherever you may be. As well as giving you peace of mind that files can be recovered, it's a good way of freeing up space on your computer from files that are rarely accessed, but you want to hold on to just in case. There are a number of different players in the market all with slightly different set-ups, price points and USPs.

Google Docs is a suite of online documents, spreadsheets and presentations with free storage of up to 1GB of material. You can pay for more if you need it. Microsoft offers Sky Drive, which has 25GB of free space and allows you to use a basic version of Office available as an online app. You can synchronise these with your computer. Amazon's free Cloud Drive service is promoted as a music application, but you can upload anything you like. Dropbox allows you to sync across all your machines, mobile devices and the cloud. Free allocation is only 2GB, but a member promotion allows you to earn more space. Boxnet has a similar offer.

Paid search

Freelancers often don't have a budget for anything, let alone marketing, but the advent of paid search theoretically lets you slug it out with the big boys. The essence of paid search is that you bid for words and phrases that you think people will use to find your products and services. So if, for example, you think that somebody is looking for a freelance graphic designer specialising in fantasy computer games, you can set up an account that bids against very specific search terms that will rank your website highly when somebody puts in that search term. In this way, you can target individuals who are searching for your specific skills and you can target geographically, with no minimum spend. You can also turn your ad spend on and off easily.

For businesses that are looking to spend money on advertising, paid search has rapidly become one of the most important tools at their disposal. Google's AdWords has the lion's share of the market – around

90% of searches. It provides a suite of tools that enables you to work out how best to utilise your budget, and the system is essentially self-service. You can set up an account with a credit or debit card. Go to www.google.co.uk/adwords to find out more.

Zamzar

Zamzar converts all kinds of graphics files from one format to another and emails you with the results. And it's free. Unfortunately the free service is funded by lots of adverts. Different packages give you fewer, or no, ads. Visit www.zamzar.com for more information.

Work–life balance

One of the key reasons that people seek to work from home is that they are looking for a better balance in their work and personal lives. Being a freelancer might seem like one way of doing this, but you have to bear in mind that your primary motivation must remain getting enough work to pay the bills and live the kind of life you want. There is nothing more stressful than struggling to constantly keep the wolf from the door.

However, for some people freelancing does create a better work–life balance. Many freelancers opt for self-employment when they start families. Working a set and relatively inflexible day does not sit well with the needs of a young family. One or both parents might want to spend less time at work and more time with their children. Legislation now allows all parents to request flexible working arrangements, but the employer does not have to accede to a request if it doesn't suit the business. With freelancing, you can more easily structure your time around other responsibilities. If you are not commuting, that extra time can be put to great use.

Without the distractions of the office, you can often get more done. Also, you can adapt your workload to suit your lifestyle. You needn't take on any more work than you think you can handle. You can also block out certain times of the day, such as the nursery/school run or even whole weeks, such as school holidays, as times when you are not available for work.

Time shift working

Working from home also allows you to shift your periods of productivity. So, for example, you may want to finish your working day early to pick up the kids, cook the evening meal, or go to a Tai Chi class. You can then work again later in the evening, making sure that you put in the hours necessary.

Of course, this approach requires a lot of discipline. It's easy to finish work early, but not so easy for some of us to pick up the reins again later in the evening. You also have to consider how time-sensitive your clients are. If there are specific times they will expect to be able to contact you, it could be tricky if you are suddenly incommunicado. If they accept your set-up and can work to it, then it's less of a problem. However, you must discuss these things with clients who may assume a 9 to 5 set-up as the norm.

Handling distractions

Working from home also has its downsides. Even if you have a separate office, it can be difficult to completely separate home and office. Every freelancer has tales of noisy toddlers coming hurtling into the room while they are in the midst of an important phone call, completely blowing the professional image you are trying to present.

In most cases you can laugh these instances off. Lots of people have children and know how hard it can be to keep them in line. However, it is probably a good idea to try and devise some guidelines that will allow you to work, without turning your house into a fun-free zone for your kids – they live there too. It is unreasonable to expect a very small child to understand why daddy or mummy can't always play with them and why they are suddenly banned from one part of the house. In such instances, it may be better to seek a workplace away from your home – renting a desk somewhere, for instance.

Dos and don'ts of working from home

Do . . .

- Do talk it over with others who live in the house. This is their living space as well, and everybody needs to agree that part of the home can be used this way.
- Do keep your workspace separate from your living space, and if possible, close a door on yourself when you're working.
- Do set a work schedule and stick to it. Work set hours, and make sure that family members know when you're working. Write a daily to-do list. Finish the day by reviewing what you have done and preparing tomorrow's list.
- Do check with your insurance and mortgage companies that your change of circumstances is okay.
- Do take into account the type of business you're running and the amount of space you'll need.
- Do be disciplined. Decide how many hours you want or need to work and then stick to them. There can be flexibility, but a regular work pattern is best.
- Do know when to switch off and relax.
- Do take advantage of working from home. If it's a nice day, adjourn to the garden with your laptop, or even take the day off if deadlines permit.
- Do create a reward system that will encourage you to be more productive. If you make it to lunchtime without checking your Facebook account, give yourself a doughnut. . . and then check Facebook.

Don't . . .

- Don't be distracted. Working from home has many potential temptations and distractions. There's always something else you could be doing, but remember that it won't pay the bills.
- Don't become isolated. Working from home can be lonely and withdraws a whole host of opportunities to pick people's brains, cross-fertilise ideas, and generally make work fun. Find other ways of staying in touch with people and make sure that you do get out and network in the real world every now and again.

- Don't forget to get plenty of storage for the office so you can quickly locate what you need.
- Don't forget to take regular breaks.
- Don't do any housework or gardening during your working day, however pressing you persuade yourself it is. It's simply an excuse not to work.
- Don't publish your home telephone number if your business is global. You don't want calls from the other side of the world waking you, and everyone else, in the middle of the night. Get a dedicated business line and a voicemail that explains your working hours. Or suggest that people contact you through email initially.

Recreating the buzz of an office

Working from home can be an isolating experience if you are used to the hubbub of being in an office. You can't exactly recreate the water cooler experience at home, but there are ways to get your social fix that will allow you to remain in touch with what's going on, and stay sane.

→ Stay in touch through regular emails and phone calls to colleagues. You haven't disappeared off the planet – you're only working from home. By staying in touch you can be sure that you will continue to be copied in on office news, gossip and happenings.

→ Join relevant associations and networking groups. There is only so much that you can do on a phone line or virtually. One face-to-face meeting can be worth 10 phone calls. People can look you in the eye and get a better idea of what you are all about. Once you've met somebody in the flesh, they are more likely to remember you. Think of the many people you have spoken to over the years and never met, compared to those where there is a more personal bond.

→ Contribute to websites and forums that are relevant to your line of work. By setting yourself up as a source of informed comment, you make yourself part of the debate. Even though you work from home, it shows you are an active participant in what's going on in your sector.

→ Dedicate a day or two a month to actually meet up with colleagues, clients and peers. Plan in advance who you want to see and what you want to achieve. Often by planning a day, you can get through more meaningful meetings than if you were in an office. You can keep the idle chit-chat to a minimum and get straight to the point of matters in hand.

→ If you are really struggling with the lack of human contact during the working day, it may make more sense to try and work in a more buzzy atmosphere, such as a freelancer-led shared office. Renting a desk does not mean that you are a wage slave again – you can set your own hours. But you may find that being among like-minded, busy people gives you the re-energising boost that you need.

→ Make full use of technology to keep yourself networked – Twitter, LinkedIn, Skype and blogs can all help you feel the social buzz.

Jelly co-working groups

A 'Jelly' is an informal co-working event where freelancers, homeworkers and small/micro business owners bring their laptop or project and work, chat and collaborate with other small business owners. The ethos of Jelly is to be accessible to all, so the venue, wi-fi and parking are provided free of charge, with small charges made for food and drink. The groups are set up around the country and encourage co-working with like-minded people in a different environment, to exchange help and advice, and maybe come up with a new idea to collaborate on.

Jelly differs from networking in that the aim is not to find new clients or to sell yourself or your business. It was established in 2006 when two New York freelancers were talking about a major drawback of working alone: namely, the lack of company. They decided to invite a group of freelancers to bring their laptops and work together in their apartment for the day, and called it Jelly as they were eating jellybeans at the time.

Jelly started in the UK in the autumn of 2009 when Lee Cottier set up events in the Bristol area. There are now more than 50 groups meeting regularly from Edinburgh to Plymouth and North Wales to Norwich. A Big Jelly mega networking event was held in March 2011 in Shropshire to bring together groups from around the country. Visit www.uk-jelly.org. uk for more information.

WANT TO KNOW MORE...

- www.flexibility.co.uk: brings together research and opinion about innovations in employment practice, organisational development, technological change and public policy.

- www.workfromhome.co.uk: resources tips and advice on homeworking.

- www.homeworking.com: advice, forums and community for homeworkers.

- www.workfromhomewisdom.com: blog of home business consultant Judy Heminsley.

- www.working5to9.co.uk: website of homeworking guru Emma Jones, author of *Spare Room Start Up*.

Help, I need more space!

If you really don't have enough room at home or anticipate a steady stream of visitors, then you will probably have to consider a completely separate space.

Many people convert a garage into an office, or put an office in the space above it. You will need to get quotes from local builders and also discuss the idea with your local planning office.

Planners generally do not object to offices at home, but will have concerns if you are expecting to receive regular visitors or employ staff. One of the biggest concerns is taking up parking space for other residents. If you need permission to build an office space, they will want to make sure you conform to health and safety regulations.

Another option is to have an office at the bottom of the garden. Converting the old garden shed is probably not the best idea but there are plenty of funky wooden 'offices' on the market. Wooden structures do not necessarily need planning permission and can provide the answer to the space issue. But make sure you have adequate, safe heating as wooden huts can be notoriously cold in winter.

WANT TO KNOW MORE...

Garden office suppliers include:

- www.boothsgardenstudios.co.uk
- www.gardenspaces.co.uk
- www.oazis-garden-office-and-studios.co.uk
- www.officeingarden.co.uk.

Shared offices

If you can't afford to splash out on a custom office, or don't want to commit to that sort of investment, you can hire desk space in a shared office or facility. This is an increasingly popular way for freelancers to find a place to work. Typically there is a flat monthly or weekly fee which gives you a desk and covers phone and internet access. It may also have a meeting space which you can book for work purposes.

Often these spaces are set up around groups of people with similar jobs, such as designers, computer programmers or PR people. One of the additional advantages of such an approach is that it gives you access to other people who you can bounce ideas off. If you are used to the hubbub of a busy office, it can be isolating to suddenly find yourself working alone. A busy office may be more conducive to getting work done. You may also encounter other freelancers who can put work your way, or who may ask you to collaborate on joint projects.

WANT TO KNOW MORE...

There are examples of shared office space all over the country. Here are a few resources for finding a space:

- www.deskspaceuk.co.uk

- www.funkyspaces.co.uk

- www.hiredeskspace.co.uk

- www.needofficespace.com

- www.officegenie.co.uk

- www.regus.co.uk.

Checklist

☑ Assess what you need to work from home.

☑ Decide where in the house you could work. If it is not an option, consider a shared workspace with other freelancers.

☑ Set a budget for your equipment.

☑ Discuss the implications of working from home with other members of your household. They live there too.

☑ Try to create a working environment that encourages you to be productive.

☑ Don't forget the health and safety considerations of working from home.

☑ Remember to stay in contact with other freelancers, colleagues and clients through social media and occasional meet ups.

☑ Make the most of work-life balance opportunities.

 **CHAPTER 5**

Getting work

📖 What's in this chapter?

Getting work is a job in its own right for any freelancer. Employers won't beat a path to your door – you will have to go out there, find them and make your pitch. This involves a whole new bunch of skills that you may not have had to use before. In this chapter we will look at:

–▷ marketing yourself to employers

–▷ social media marketing

–▷ networking

–▷ pitching your work

–▷ getting commissioned.

Now what?

So you've finally made the jump to freelancing. You've resigned from your old job, registered as self-employed, and set up in your new all-singing all-dancing office. Now what?

As you sit at your desk on the first day as a freelancer, a moment of panic can set in as you ponder what you've done. There is no longer a pay cheque automatically coming your way at the end of each month. From now on you will be responsible for generating work for yourself and chasing payment.

That's quite a daunting prospect. But don't panic – this is only wasted energy. Every freelancer feels like this at the beginning, and it's hardly surprising. It is a big change to go from the comforting certainties of 9 to 5 work to the more seat-of-the-pants world of freelancing.

You will often hear established freelancers use the phrase 'feast or famine' to describe the flow of work. By this they mean that there is either too much work or absolutely none. Getting used to this state of affairs, and doing what you can to smooth out the peaks and the troughs, is another skill you are going to have to master.

Welcome to your new world of work.

Where to start

In an ideal world you should start your plans before you actually go freelance. As has been stated in Chapter 3, your existing (or previous) employer and contacts are the best initial source of work. They know you and your capabilities and, providing you haven't been a complete waste of space to them, there is no reason why they shouldn't at least listen to a proposal from you on how you can lighten the load by taking some work off their hands.

Don't simply expect them to hand over work out of the goodness of their hearts. Make the business case to them why they should outsource to you.

⇨ You can do it more cost-effectively.

⇨ You have expertise that they don't have in-house.

⇨ You can free up resources that can be better deployed elsewhere.

⇨ You can do a better job than they can manage in-house.

There is no one way to track down work. You need to be alert to the possibilities of getting work at all times. Somebody you bump into in the street may be a potential client. Don't be embarrassed about mentioning to somebody that you can supply services to them, or about asking them if they currently use freelancers. They may not have considered this approach, in which case you can introduce them to the many and varied benefits of using a freelancer.

Spread the risk

It is important that you try to develop a broad portfolio of clients. The obvious danger in being over-reliant on a single client is the high degree of risk it exposes you to. If that company dispenses with your services or goes bust, then you are up the creek without a paddle.

When you start out, don't be too sniffy about the kind of work that you accept. We would all love to work on the most exciting, creative and impressive projects, but the reality is that quite often that's the sort of work that in-house staff will want to do. And who can blame them?

You may find that you are offered quite dull, routine work that nobody else in the company really wants to do. Them's the breaks I'm afraid.

What you should remember is that by doing a good job on this kind of work, you may position yourself as a reliable freelancer who can be trusted to do a good job on something more exciting at some point in the future. However, if you come over all diva-ish and rule yourself out for no better reason than you think it's beneath you, in all likelihood you can kiss goodbye to being offered work from that company again.

And maybe not just that company. People move around from one company to another, so news of your bad attitude can travel too. Nurtured properly, a freelance career is just that – a career that you can try and develop. Don't nip it in the bud at the early stage by ruling out work. There is no unlimited supply of sources of work. You will be amazed as you go through your career how often you bump into the same people. Make sure that they remember you for good reasons.

Reasons to turn work down

Supermodel Linda Evangelista famously claimed she didn't wake up for for less than $10,000 a day. You might not be quite as lucky as that, but don't feel you have to accept all jobs. There are perfectly acceptable reasons for turning down work.

- You may be too busy to take something on. Think of this as a quality control measure. A rushed job can end up failing to deliver what a client wants. The client doesn't really care how busy you are, only that you give them what they need. Don't take it on if you can't deliver.
- You may not have the particular skills that are required for a job. There is nothing wrong with working a bit outside of your comfort zone, and you may surprise yourself by taking on a piece of work that seemed beyond your experience. However, if it seems way beyond your capacity, politely turn it down and explain why. If you know somebody else who can do it, suggest them as an alternative. You'll gain brownie points from the client and the grateful freelancer.
- The rate is not acceptable to you. Rates are not set in stone, and there may be times when you have to be flexible: if, for example, a client's budget is really limited, or your work schedule is looking a bit empty. At such times you may feel that you have to accept a lower rate for a job than you normally would. Also, if the job is sufficiently interesting in its own right – perhaps it will provide you with some valuable experience that will round out your CV a bit and help you pick up work in another area in future. However, as a general rule, try to stick to a rate that you think is fair. Rates can go down very quickly if you let them, but they only rise slowly, and usually with a great deal of effort.

Marketing yourself

While working for another company, you may have given little thought to marketing. Work seemed to arrive magically from somewhere, and you simply performed your role and were paid for it. However, the company you worked for will have derived that work by developing clients through the process of marketing.

In some cases companies don't actually have anybody who is trained as a marketer, or who would even consider themselves to be one. This doesn't matter. Some of the best marketers are people with an instinctive feel for what their market wants and who can then go about supplying it. Think of people like Lord Alan Sugar, Sir Richard Branson and Yo Sushi's Simon Woodroffe. They are entrepreneurs who have developed businesses through hard work and gut instinct, but they have also used marketing nous, even if they would not necessarily call it that.

What is marketing?

The Chartered Institute of Marketing (CIM) defines marketing as:

> 'The management process responsible for identifying, anticipating and satisfying customer requirements profitably.'

In a nutshell, it means you have to work out what potential clients want and what they will pay, and go about trying to offer them that service.

Marketers sometimes talk about the four Ps of marketing. These are:

1. product: what you offer

2. price: the rate that you can charge for your services

3. place as a freelancer: this refers to where your work comes from

4. promotion: how you go about making people aware of what you offer.

In recent years, the four Ps approach has been regarded as limited in describing the marketing process. Some practitioners talk about a fifth P of people, and the CIM now talks of seven Ps with the addition of process and physical evidence. However many Ps you decide on, your marketing is made up of the interplay of these elements. This is referred to as the marketing mix.

Too often, people think of marketing in terms of its outcomes, such as glossy print ads or TV commercials. However, it is better to think of marketing as a process, and one that should be embedded into your business from the very start. A good way of doing this is to create a marketing plan detailing where you are, where you want to go and how you are going to get there.

Building a marketing plan means setting down a blueprint for effective marketing. It can also be a useful way of determining where the business is heading.

Product and pricing

The key to this is research. The more thorough your marketing plan, the better. If your business is going to operate within a specific locality, will the market support it? For example, if you plan to freelance as a wedding photographer, how many already exist, what type of service do they offer and what are their prices like? How do they position themselves – cheap and cheerful, traditional style shot, or artistic and off the wall? Will the locality support another photographer or is the area already saturated? Check out rivals' prices, too, and position your service accordingly.

You can use the same approach to introduce new services or determine whether it is viable to expand into other markets. Is there a niche for the service or do competitors have the market sewn up? How do you plan to sell the service – directly or via an agency? What distribution method will you use?

Position

This means creating an identity for your business. You want to stand out from the crowd and be distinctive, so you may want to develop an identity that is instantly recognisable. Many freelancers will simply use their own name and do not really need to go down the branding route. However, even here, defining your position can help the market understand what you do, the services you offer and help you promote yourself accordingly.

If you have created a limited company or want to promote greater awareness, you may want a specific brand for your business. A brand is more than a logo and a creative name. It is the emotional and psychological relationship you have with your customers. As such, it is made up of the expectations that they might have of you from past work or from peer recommendation. A brand is business shorthand that conveys what your business is all about, and it should contain a certain truth about your business.

What's in a name?

A name like Trotters International Traders is not a very reliable brand name, as Del Boy and Rodney never made it any further than Peckham market with their business aspirations. Similarly, a brand name like Total Communications Solutions is not a good brand for a freelance journalist who does a bit of corporate writing but doesn't really know anything about developing or implementing a communications strategy.

When creating a brand, keep it simple and keep it truthful. Think what your business's brand values are and try to reflect them in your brand. If you are creative and zany, don't try and present yourself as a traditional, po-faced business person. Let your personality come through.

A business name is important and should reflect the value of the product or the service. Ideally it should be original and punchy if possible. Avoid naff names – it reflects poorly on the business and gives it an unprofessional appearance. How many hairdressers do you know called Snips, Cut n Curl or Blow Dry? Too many.

Before choosing a name, check the business section at your local library, google it or get in touch with Companies House to make sure you are not planning to use a name that is already in use.

Creating your brand identity

To create the brand identity, find a good local designer who can come up with letterheads, business cards and packaging. Designers can also be found in the business section of the local library.

Design is one of those curious trades which everybody thinks they can do themselves. While anybody can have an idea for a brand, designers are professionals who can develop your idea or create a unique identity and professional appearance for your business. A good local designer need not be expensive and may be a freelancer too, and thus sympathetic to your needs and ambitions.

Promotion

Promotion is the visible part of marketing for many people. It is like the upper 10% of the iceberg. Customer targeting is the first and most important step in planning any kind of promotional activity. You really need to know who your customers are before wasting any money on marketing communication.

Lord Leverhulme, the founder of Unilever, famously said:

> 'Half the money I spend on advertising is wasted, and the problem is I don't know which half.'

Mind you, he was a millionaire. As a freelancer, such profligacy would be crazy. Try and answer these questions.

- → What kind of people buy or will buy your product?
- → What do your best customers tend to have in common?
- → Can you reach all of your customers through the same communication channels?
- → Do customers fall into different groups?
- → Are there different buying circumstances, for example, planned, impulse or special occasion?

By answering these questions you will discover who your customers are. The next step is finding effective channels to communicate your message. These fall into three categories: media advertising (above-the-line), non-media communications (below-the-line) and public relations.

Media advertising consists of television, radio, the press, cinema, outdoor and transport. Non-media consists of sales literature, direct marketing, sponsorship, sales promotion and point of sale. Public relations involves a range of activities which attempt to create a positive attitude towards your company or products.

Marketing techniques

Once you have determined who your customers are, you can start to try to contact them. As a freelancer, you will want to use the most cost-effective marketing techniques. Note that these are not necessarily the cheapest. Even low cost marketing is a waste of money if it doesn't achieve cut through with your target market.

There are many different techniques and channels that you can use as a freelancer to promote your services. Some of the most common are outlined below.

Word of mouth

The majority of freelancers find word of mouth, or WoM as it is sometimes called, their best marketing tool. Quite simply, people who you have worked for and who like your work pass on your details to others. You may think that there isn't much you can do to engender WoM, but there are ways to make it work harder for you.

For new clients, try and over-deliver on the early jobs to show them what you can do for them. New clients are the most impressionable – remember the old adage about never getting a second chance to make a first impression. They are looking closely at your service, so give them every reason to be delighted. Seek out feedback after the job is over. This will allow you to gauge how satisfied they have been and also give a gentle prod about your availability for future projects, both from them and from others.

Don't neglect more established customers. Try and work out who are the more satisfied with a little customer satisfaction survey. This can take the form of brief chat, or you could devise a simple questionnaire on a tool like Survey Monkey (www.surveymonkey.com) which you could include with your next invoice.

Approach the more positive customers for a review or recommendation on sites such as LinkedIn or a ratings site such as Yelp. You can then include links on your website or in emails to potential customers. With digital channels, WoM can now spread much further and more quickly.

PR

The Chartered Institute of Public Relations (CIPR) defines PR as the discipline which looks after reputation, with the aim of earning understanding and support and influencing opinion and behaviour. It is the planned and sustained effort to establish and maintain goodwill and mutual understanding between an organisation and its customers.

For freelancers, it is one of the most cost-effective ways of promoting what you do and creating awareness of your expertise. The great thing about PR is that it can be effectively free and it is one of the marketing disciplines that can be handled in-house.

PR may have an *Absolutely Fabulous* image of air kissing and free lunches, but at its heart it is about communication and getting your story out to a carefully selected target audience. This may be the media, who you hope will print your story and make it more widely read among your potential clients. It could also be a direct communication with a group of potential clients, such as meeting them at a trade show.

Reputation matters

PR is about creating and preserving a good reputation among the people who matter to your business: customers, suppliers and industry peers. PR offers an opportunity to highlight your freelance company where your name is unfamiliar. You can build and sustain your image by gaining editorial in your local press, trade websites and magazines, speaking at events or providing commentary on topical events.

You will have to develop a sense of what is newsworthy for your target media. This varies by publication or news channel. Some may be interested in personality-type pieces about how you made it. Others may be solely focused on hard news. Find out what kind of stories they want and set about trying to deliver this. You will also find out who to target on a publication. Although you may think that the editor is the first port of call, the reality is that in many media outlets you won't get near him or her as they are too busy to deal with speculative calls. The news editor or individual reporters with particular specialisms are often a better bet.

How to write a press release

If you are launching a company or a product a press release is not a bad way to go about it, because a new company is generally hard news and the press likes new things.

Press releases should have the look and feel of a news item you would read in a publication. At first glance, most press releases look simple and harmless enough but even the biggest companies agonise over them.

Make sure the wording is correct, the message is clear and direct, and the correct information is provided so that a journalist will be able to use it, even if they do not contact a member of your company or public relations team.

Your release should convey a sense of importance but not seem over-hyped. You want to provide information about your firm in a newsy format, not a marketing letter. 'It needs to be factual, not opinion,' suggests the Institute of Public Relations. Besides, if your announcement is worth sending a release out about, it can probably stand on its own without marketing hype.

An example of a press release is featured in Appendix 2. As a rule all press releases should answer the journalist's five basic questions of:

1. who?

2. what?

3. where?

4. why?

5. how?

This will require you to put yourself in the shoes of a journalist and the chances are, the answering those questions will give you a clearer idea of what you want to write. A punchy headline should be included that matches the release's first sentence, or lead, as those in the trade call it. The headline should be factual. It shouldn't try to make a joke or be smart.

A date line should precede the start of the text. The date line is usually in bold or capitalised and tells the journalist where it is being released and what date it is being released, for example: London, 2 September 2012.

The first sentence should be direct, relate what is going on, convey a level of importance of the news and start off with the name of your firm. As a matter of preference the sentences in the release should be kept as short as possible.

Journalists write in a style called the 'inverted pyramid' and your releases should do the same. The inverted pyramid style of writing requires that the most important information is provided first within the story, rather than deeper in the text.

The idea is, that you should be able to cut from the bottom of the story and no matter where you cut from you can still get a sense for what is going on – even if the only thing that is used is the first sentence.

A quote, or recorded statement from an officer of the company, should be included within the text. It's always useful to have a quote to give a more 'human' side to the content and to lend some authority. A quote can both personalise the release and give the journalist an idea of who to speak with. Most journalists will seek their own quotes by following up releases with interviews, but having a quote gives journalists the option to use it.

The release should close with an editor's note paragraph that describes your company. This is where you can put in some marketing by underscoring your services, experience and uniqueness.

Contact details for journalists who want to find out more about what is happening can either go at the top of the release or the bottom. All releases should be as specific and targeted as possible as to who they are contacting at a newspaper as the days of using blanket press releases, announcements not posted to anyone or any publication in particular are over. Journalists get inundated with hundreds of releases and, in truth, most end up in the bin because they aren't directed to a person.

Direct marketing

As its name suggests, direct marketing is the act of marketing directly to someone on a one to one basis. As such, it can take many forms: letters, email, inserts in newspapers or magazines, door to door leaflets, instant messaging, even picking up the phone to somebody.

The crux of direct marketing is that you use the information you glean about potential clients to target them with pinpoint accuracy. So if, for example, you are a private tutor in East Anglia, you may only be interested in targeting the parents of A level English students within 15 miles of Norwich. Direct marketing allows you to do this.

Obtaining new clients is essential to the success of any business. Direct marketing gives you the opportunity to reach the most relevant audience for your product or service and create a direct relationship with them as an individual. Direct marketing can also be used to develop an ongoing relationship with customers to maximise their loyalty, value and consequently profitability over time.

It's all about data

Data is the crucial element in successful direct marketing. Data can be any piece of information that you have about a customer that helps you to build up a better picture of them, such as:

- name
- address
- telephone number
- email
- job title
- number of people in the company
- their transaction history, i.e. how much business they have done with you.

You can obtain data in two main ways: by collecting it yourself or by buying it. You can buy data from list brokers who can work out the type of data that you need and match it to a list, or directly from data owners such as publishers of magazines or catalogue companies who collect data on their customers.

When buying data, the quality, accuracy and relevance of the list of potential customers used is one of the most important factors for a direct marketing campaign. The more thought put into its selection, the more accurate the targeting will be and the more responsive the campaign.

Firstly you must decide which product or service you wish to promote and then choose a list of the audience for which this is most suited. The list is selected from a wide range of relevant options, such as area, industry type, turnover, size of company, job function, and so on.

Channel and message

When carrying out your direct marketing campaign, you have to carefully consider both the method of delivery and the message itself. Different groups of people have different preferences about how they are contacted. For example, a young, technically literate audience might have no problems receiving a text message from you. An older group might prefer a letter in the post.

Equally important is the message. Given that the majority of direct marketing is dismissed as junk mail by recipients, you have to cut to the chase quickly with your message. Make it relevant to the target audience, make it simple and easy to understand, and outline the benefit of your offer (e.g. a free consultation if they reply within 30 days). The message should close with an understanding of what is required of the recipient of the offer (e.g. they complete the enclosed form, phone the company, visit a website, etc.).

Campaigns should also be carried out in controllable quantities. If the campaign is too large, it carries the risk of the response being too great to cope with. A smaller distribution is easier to handle and responses can be dealt with more efficiently and professionally. As a freelancer, the last thing you want to do is to turn away a customer because you have overloaded yourself.

If you are going to do a lot of direct marketing, it is well worth equipping yourself with some of the skills of the craft, such as copywriting for direct marketing. The Institute of Direct and Digital marketing (IDM) runs practical courses on many aspects of direct marketing (www.theidm.com).

Email marketing

One specific area of direct marketing that deserves closer consideration is the use of email. As the cheapest way to run a direct marketing campaign, it is the channel most likely to be used by freelancers to contact existing and potential customers. However, just because it is cheap does not mean that you should run riot, bombarding prospects with electronic messages. This can lead to people being so hacked off with you that they delete your message without even opening it. Don't risk becoming regarded as a spammer just because you haven't followed a few simple rules.

Email is a very cheap medium to reach a lot of potential customers. You can create awareness quickly and, if you build a strong message, you may find better responses from emails than hard copy mailers. It enables you to build newsworthy and up to the minute offers, responding quickly to changing market conditions. For example, if there is a flu bug doing the rounds, you might want to drop clients an email reminding them of your availability as cover for ill staff.

As with other types of direct mail, make sure that your email is relevant to the recipient. Don't send it out to all and sundry if it is only likely to appeal to a select few. Don't feel the need to supply reams of copy with additional detail. You can include a link to a website for more detail. Concentrate on getting people interested with the email first.

You need to decide whether to use html or text format. The former allows more designer touches but may put off some people. The latter cuts to the message but may be a bit bland. Which suits your audience best? You can send emails through Outlook but functionality is limited. There are lots of free email packages you can try, such as Mailchimp, Graphicmail and dotMailer. Ask what colleagues are using and what they think of it.

And remember to keep it legal. Simply put, if you are emailing out marketing messages, then either the recipient must have agreed to receive the message or you already have them on your list as a legitimate buying customer. You must provide a current address for the recipient to use to contact you to withdraw their consent for mailings.

Search engine marketing

Marketing these days is all about being found by your customers. Whether you are Apple or Joe Bloke, a freelance plumber, people will expect to be able to find out about you, make contact with you, and even do business with you, online. For this reason, search rankings have become all important.

Your search ranking is where you are found on a page of search results on sites such as Google or Bing, when somebody puts in your name or a relevant term for your business. Search engine optimisation (SEO) is the process of enhancing the quantity and quality of traffic to a website through search engines. SEO practice dates back to the mid-90s when search engines were first organising webpages. It is becoming ever more important to businesses as a means of improving traffic to their sites. In general, the higher the site appears in the search results list, the more visitors it will receive via the search engine, so aim to get your website as high on the list as possible.

Surveys have found that most people don't look beyond the first page of search results, and many don't look beyond the top half of the page. Getting your site into this slot is therefore crucial. However, many firms still fail to take steps to improve their search engine rankings, despite the fact that Google remains the first port of call for most people looking for goods and services.

There are a number of ways by which a freelancer can optimise their search ranking. These include editing the content on their site and creating more relevant content that customers are more likely to search for. It is also sometimes necessary to change the HTML coding of the website in order to increase its relevance to specific keywords and to remove any barriers to search engine activities.

Basic SEO practice

There are various things to consider before starting search engine optimisation for your website. Your company's website is its shop window. It's crucial that you consider and start to implement SEO best practice right from the design stage. Trying to optimise your website for search engines once it is live and in use is a more complex, and ultimately costly, task.

Take time to consider which search engines are worth targeting, and what you're offering your target audience. Google, Yahoo! and Bing are the only search engines you need to worry about. Currently Google accounts for 65%–70% of search engine activity, so you could just focus your attention on Google.

SEO is more of an art than a science. The algorithms used by search engines, especially Google, are shrouded in secrecy and constantly changing, so you can never guarantee your position at the top of a search page. However, there are some basic rules to apply when optimising your site.

→ Consider the content of your site first of all. Think about exactly what you're offering and how relevant your content and web copy is.

→ Get your business on Google maps: it's quick and easy to do, and is a good promotional tool.

→ Keyword research: start by typing in the most basic phrase for your service and then go from there. Google Keyword Tools can tell you how many people have searched for a particular keyword, and also how many other sites have used that keyword. Going for the most popular will make it harder to get to the top of the search ranking, so you may want to tailor your keywords to fit your business more specifically, e.g. 'blue swimwear', as opposed to just 'swimwear'. Keyword Tools will also give you a list of similar phrases that people look for, and how popular they are. Through this tool you can create a keyword library that contains phrases you think are most likely to generate searches to your site. It is better to focus on a small number of keywords and channel your efforts on promoting those.

→ Always make sure you use simple language and don't use abbreviations for words.

→ Produce regular content: build your content around the keywords. Write it so that it flows well. Google is looking for natural density (how often a keyword or phrase appears on a page, expressed as a percentage), so if it reads well while using the keywords then it should be the correct density. You need to have enough content to show you are an authority on the subject, but this does not have to be located on your homepage.

→ Each page on your website should have a descriptive URL which should tell Google what your business does.

Social media marketing

Although Google still reigns supreme online, search is not the all-conquering power is once was. People are now finding sites through social media feeds, blogs, and podcasts. For freelancers in particular, these kinds of links are becoming ever more important.

Facebook, Twitter, LinkedIn and YouTube all offer freelancers distinct opportunities to connect with a vast network of potential clients and to raise their own profile. All of the sites are relatively easy to use, and you can build a profile across sites that can be interlinked. As you start to operate across a number of social media platforms, you can utilise a product such as Tweetdeck or Hootsuite to integrate your social media output.

Facebook

By far the most widely used social networking site, Facebook offers direct access to more than 900 million users, and it's growing all the time. Although it's seen by many as more of a social site, it presents a huge range of opportunities for freelancers in the online community. Facebook is a platform where you can interact with current and potential customers, and where you can promote your services.

Facebook has taken steps to actively encourage businesses to use its service, by offering initiatives such as Facebook adverts and Facebook Pages. You can set up a company profile or groups and message boards where customers can converge to discuss with one another the service they have received. Like other social media sites, the key here is openness, and you must be willing to give up a certain degree of control to customers.

Keeping content interesting and relevant is crucial to any social media page, and Facebook is no exception. To attract and retain followers or fans, you need to offer exciting content that stands out from the crowd. Consider different forms of content, such as video, audio, pictures or blogs that would most appeal to your target audience. Facebook can also be used as a market research tool, through which companies can poll their fans and measure their reaction to new ideas.

Once your Page is set up, start off small by inviting friends and current customers, who will then invite their friends and so on. Social media is an extremely viral form of communication, so don't expect to have thousands of fans overnight.

Top tips for using Facebook

⇥ Post regular updates on your wall: it is important to keep content fresh and interesting. But try not to add too many updates because content overload will overwhelm your fans and swamp their newsfeed pages.

⇥ Make use of video or images: keep your page visual as this helps to engage your audience.

⇥ Carry out market research: Facebook offers a free platform for market research. Poll your fans to find out what they think of your ideas.

⇥ Respond to comments: make sure you reply to questions or comments posted by fans and start developing a dialogue with them. Similarly, reply to criticism, don't ignore it.

⇥ Start discussion groups: encourage conversation about your business. This is an effective way to boost brand awareness, and you can educate followers about your product or service.

⇥ Use Facebook ads to increase your fan base: although it's no substitute for proper engagement, it can help boost fan numbers.

⇥ Share blog posts: if you have a blog make sure you share the latest posts on your Facebook fan page.

⇥ Avoid over-commercialisation: when sharing interesting product news or offers, try not to be too profit-focused. Social media sites are not merely another sales platform and being overly commercial is a guaranteed way to deter fans.

Twitter

The micro-blogging site has about 500 million users worldwide, which lags behind Facebook's 900 million. However, when it comes to promotion, Twitter is arguably more effective because of its openness. Public Twitter updates are available for anyone to see, making it an attractive platform. You can also protect your tweets so that they are only visible to approved followers.

Twitter can be used by companies in a variety of ways. For freelancers, it's an extension of your other social media efforts and can serve to draw attention to your content on other platforms. Recruitment and customer services are two examples of how small firms are using Twitter, as well as the obvious tweeting of company news or industry insights. Many businesses forget to retweet and reply to other peoples' tweets. This is a crucial way to build a community and gain influence.

Freelancers can also tweet details of their latest projects. For example, a web designer might tweet a link to a new site he has produced. He could even direct people to the Beta version and ask for their comments on usability or overall design.

With Twitter, it is even more important that you are available to engage, because it is an immediate channel. It is quick and easy to set up alerts to inform you when people have mentioned you or something of interest to you, allowing you to connect with that person on a more intimate level.

Top tips for businesses using Twitter

→ Keep it simple: with only 140 characters at your disposal, it can be difficult to convey your message in a concise way. To keep followers engaged, tweets must be clear and to the point.

→ Engage conversationally with followers, not in corporate speak.

→ Encourage followers to click your link: whenever possible you should include a link to your website in your tweets. By keeping tweets interesting you will persuade more click-throughs.

→ Reflect your personality or brand through your tweets: don't be afraid to use a lighter tone on Twitter. You are more likely to build relationships with your followers if you appear more approachable.

→ Create a list of useful contacts: use Twitter Lists to assemble a record of key people in your industry, including useful groups and relevant people.

→ Reply to tweets swiftly: always try to respond as quickly as possible to any messages directed to your business. This will help engage your followers.

⇢ Use web analytics: link your Twitter account to a web analytics service to identify what drives web traffic, and then how likely this traffic is to convert into customers.

⇢ Ask questions: this is a great way to encourage engagement with your followers. You could ask for feedback on your latest products or services, or even content ideas for your blog.

⇢ Be original: try not to constantly tweet about the same thing. The most successful brands on Twitter provide a good balance of diverse tweets, some serious, some purely promotional, and some of a lighter tone, to keep followers interested.

⇢ Update your profile look: keep your Twitter page fresh by using different colours and pictures.

LinkedIn

If virtual teams, brought together like the 'A-Team' for one-off projects, are one future of work, LinkedIn is Hannibal, providing the connections and pulling the strings. The site is the largest professional social network in the world. At present it boasts 150 million members worldwide, four million of whom are from the UK. LinkedIn claims one third of British professionals are now signed up.

It's the large business audience that sets LinkedIn apart from other social media sites. There are currently more than one million company profiles on LinkedIn including 100,000 in the UK alone. Professionals can use it to gain access to insight and expertise, as well as a sales channel to promote their business. By building up solid connections, members can seek advice on strategies and share information with other companies.

No matter how busy your company is, LinkedIn claims it can give small businesses the power of big businesses. Freelancers can reach further by accessing information in any field, something they would otherwise not have the resources for. See pp 150–152 for how to build up a professional network on LinkedIn.

Top tips for businesses using LinkedIn

⇢ Start discussions: interact with other professionals and companies and keep content relevant and interesting.

-> Fill out your profile and insert lots of keywords about what you do, where you are located and what your services are.

-> Create links to different pages of your site.

-> Look for recommendations: you can display testimonials and endorsements from previous clients and customers. It's a powerful indicator of jobs well done.

-> The 'answers' tool can be used to ask a specific question aimed at a particular industry. This is a great way to find out information and opens up a plethora of detailed responses.

-> You can use the 'direct ads' section where people can post adverts on the network and then target them to certain industries of their choice.

-> Be conscious that it is a network for professionals. The key is to build relationships, but this is not meant to be a social platform where people can organise their evening plans with friends.

YouTube

Founded in 2005, YouTube is by far the world's most popular video hosting website. This free-to-use site has approximately 24 hours of video content uploaded every minute, and its mass-market audience means it's an ideal marketing channel.

In order to maximise YouTube's marketing potential, you must think creatively. With millions of videos to choose from, it's easy to get lost in the crowd. Therefore, think about what exactly you want your content to portray and the message you are sending out to viewers, because this will reflect on how you are perceived. You might decide that you have nothing that is visually stimulating enough to add to the online world.

However, there are still a number of features on YouTube that can help build brand awareness. You can share and embed videos on websites or blogs. Videos can be rated by viewers, and can also be commented upon, all of which may have a positive effect on you – so long as the feedback is positive.

Top tips for businesses using YouTube

⟿ Think about video content: many videos can be boring and repetitive, so think carefully about what will be most interesting and relevant to your audience. Also consider whether your video is aimed at informing your established customers or if it is more of a sales tool for potential customers.

⟿ Where else is your video going? Consider posting your video on other social networks and also think about whether it would be of interest to journalists or bloggers.

⟿ Create your own channel: YouTube creates a profile channel every time someone posts a video. Viewers can subscribe to that channel and then businesses can send out emails to those subscribers. Make sure your videos direct visitors to your site by including your web address and other contact information.

⟿ Respond to comments: make sure you reply to all comments, whether good or bad.

⟿ Engage with the YouTube community: check out other content and rate your favourite videos. You can even make suitable 'friends' to build your community presence.

⟿ Keep up to date with YouTube's news: stay on top of changes to the site. The official YouTube blog is a good place to follow the community's news.

⟿ Keep track of where your video has been hosted: it may have been embedded on other websites or blogs. Make sure you keep on top of conversations about your video.

⟿ Include clear titles and descriptions for your video: this will help increase traffic. Pick your keywords carefully so they fit your subject area and niche, and so they draw in a wide audience. Video plays an important role in search, so make sure Google can find yours easily by including lots of relevant keywords.

⟿ Keep videos short and snappy: viewers are unlikely to sit through very long videos.

The important thing with all social media is that you don't give up after the first attempt doesn't yield great interest. Just as in the offline world, building up relationships takes time, and creating a well-regarded destination on these sites takes time and effort. The most effective social marketing strategy is to combine all of the sites and try to make them all reflect the same communication from your personal brand.

Social media tips

The key elements to remember when shaping your social media plan.

Audience

To get people talking about you, you have to know all the background. Research your typical customer – what are their online habits? What do they talk about online? What's the tone of voice? Are people already talking about you? Once you have a clear idea where your audience is and what they're saying, you'll know where you should have a presence.

Conversation platforms

Don't join Facebook or set up a Twitter profile just because you think you should. Think about who your audience is. You should be engaging on the sites that your customers are on.

Your presence

Your website is the face of your brand and often the hub of your business, and so it should be the hub of social media as well. Make sure all your social media channels are integrated and on the front page. Try to drive people back to your website, but, equally, keep your content 'out there' and circulating. You should be integrating with your customers' online lives.

Building followers

Unfortunately there's no quick, easy way to do this. It's all about having something interesting to say and giving your audience what they want. Chances are, unless you're Apple or the BBC, people aren't going to be interested in internal appointments and financial figures – they want to know about the people behind the company. Be personable, approachable, funny and smart. Promotions and giveaways for your social media fans can help boost your numbers, but it's your personality that will keep them there.

Integration

Social media is not an isolated channel. If you're not prepared to integrate social media with your overall marketing, digital, search, and/or customer service strategies, you're not ready for social media. Identify how the social media conversations you're having can be fed back into the business.

Measurement

Social media is highly measurable, but only if you're using the right tools. Make sure you've incorporated Google Analytics to track conversions from your social media sites. If you're using any social media monitoring tools, such as Radian 6, set out some benchmarks from the beginning. It's not just about sales – you also have to think about brand perception, buzz and sentiment.

Advertising

You might think that advertising is the last road that a freelancer would want to go down, but there are options that make it affordable for a one-man band. Not all advertising entails shoots on exotic locations or celebrity endorsement. For smaller players, there are ways you can make it work for you.

Advertising is simply a commercial message that is bought to be placed in media of some sort: newspaper, magazine, TV, poster slot, cinema, website or radio are the main ones. There are all sorts of more exotic media choices including toilet ads, taxi ads, and even ads placed on cows. It all works in the same basic way. You pay a fee based on the exposure your ad will get to a particular audience. The more exposure, and the more targeted the media seller can guarantee, the higher the price he can charge.

This may all sound expensive, but think about some of the less expensive options that are out there. As with any type of marketing, the first step is to assess who your target market is and what type of media they are likely to consume.

Stay close to home

Something as simple as the classified section in your local newspaper could be a good place to start. Rates will be fairly manageable and you can try it for a limited period to see what kind of response you get. Local magazines are also a good bet, as they are geographically targeted and may also run local business focus features that you could advertise around. Generally speaking, for business advertising, unless you are a regular advertiser it is a good idea to try and advertise around a feature or section that has some relevance to your service. So, if you are a freelance interior designer, the homes section or a specific feature on the benefits of interior design would be a good place to advertise.

When buying advertising space you will be quoted a price from a ratecard. In most cases you will be able to negotiate a lower rate. Hardly anybody pays the ratecard rate, and in these times of advertising depression, rates are even harder to sustain. Bargain hard.

Consider free media options as well. Something as simple as a poster put in your local library or shopping centre can pay dividends. If you have leaflets about your business you may also find other local businesses that are prepared to display them. Similar low cost options include postcards and business cards that can be left with other companies.

We are all bombarded with commercial messages these days, so try to make your advertising stand out. This does not mean you have to be clever or funny. It is more important that your message is clear and that you convey it simply to your audience. You want them to understand immediately what you are offering them and what you want them to do, rather than leave them scratching their heads.

Directories

There are many ways of advertising your business, but one of the most cost-effective is by using traditional and new directory listing services.

→ **Printed directories:** publications such as the BT phonebook are used by local and national customers.

→ **Online directories:** enable consumers to search for businesses in geographical locations by business name or sector via sites such as Smilelocal, MoreUK.com and thephonebook.com, as well as hundreds of specialist trade and professional portals.

→ **Online search tools:** help businesses get themselves found via search engines such as Google, Yahoo! and Bing.

Some people think traditional directory listings such as printed or online directories are a dying trend, but research shows that consumers still rely on printed directories to search for local services such as solicitors, florists and garage services. And it's not just printed directories which are being used effectively to help businesses get noticed and generate new business. Online directories are increasingly becoming the first port of call.

There are also lots of specialist directories that cater for freelancers in particular sectors, such as photography, design, consultancy or journalism. Find out about these and how you can be included. Some may be free to members of an organisation, so you may have to join up. Others charge a small fee for listing, or for an enhanced listing. This can be worth considering, as it will give you greater prominence among the many other freelancers who are included. When putting together an entry, try to sell yourself by including details of your experience, your specialisms, and clients you have worked for.

Print or online?

So which medium should you use – print or online? The answer is a bit of both. And the good news is that there are a number of free services out there for businesses to take advantage of, so it doesn't have to cost the earth.

→ Printed and online search directories allow businesses one free listing, with the opportunity to display their business more prominently for a small charge.

→ Web presence: the more web presence a company has, the more likely a customer will find them... which is why using social media such as Twitter, Facebook, blogs and forums all help in addition to directory listings and having an amazing website.

↠ Online search marketing can help you get noticed online simply by maximising your online presence, so that potential customers are pushed to you rather than having to pull customers in.

↠ Keywords: the more times relevant keywords associated with a business appear on the web, the more likely it is that a customer will see that business name in online search results.

Recommendations

Recommendation is another route to getting work. Use your contacts to try to connect with other potential clients. This is the basis of social media such as LinkedIn, but we've been doing it in the real world for years. A mention from a friend that, 'Fred is a great guy and a reliable freelancer. I've known him for years,' will work wonders for you and could fast forward you to the front of the queue. At any rate, it will get you on the radar of firms more quickly if you are recommended by a mutual business contact.

Once you have the opportunity, it's down to you to convert it. Approach each individual prospective client with a strong case and proposal, and point out exactly how you can help their business. As an alternative to time-consuming and ineffective cold calling, referrals could work for you.

Personality counts when pitching ideas. Whether emailing an idea, speaking to somebody on the phone, or meeting them face to face, aim to be as professional as possible. It is a good idea to keep your personality fairly neutral until you have an idea of what sort of client you are dealing with. The last thing you want is for them to go off you before you have had a chance to assess your pitch. Don't be too over the top or 'matey'. Stick to the script of who you are, what you do, what your experience is and what you can offer the business.

Successful networking

Freelancing isn't just about sitting in your perfect home office and plotting your business empire over cups of tea. Sometimes you actually have to get out there and hustle for business. Although it would be nice to have the phone ring constantly with offers of work, the reality is that you have to keep reminding people who you are, what you do, and what you can do for them. Networking, whether in the real world, or increasingly in the virtual world, is the way to do it.

Networking can help you make the right contacts, build closer working relationships, improve your visibility and obtain valuable information. It's also about selling yourself and your services, but often not in a hard-edged way. Networking is a more subtle exercise than that, but it can still result in real business gains. However, you shouldn't expect immediate results.

Give the solitary nature of freelancing, networking is vitally important. Without it, you lose the opportunity to share experiences with other like-minded people facing similar problems and issues – from the effects of legislation to the best way to use social media.

It can take years to build an extensive business network. But the benefits of having instant expertise on tap are huge. Once you can count on people as contacts, the solution to any business problem – or advice on how to tackle it – is a phone call away.

Think of networking as the proactive marketing of your freelance business. In cases where companies prefer to buy through word of mouth referrals, networking can be more effective than advertising as a way of winning business. It can also reduce the need for cold calling.

Of course, networking isn't anything new. People have joined golf clubs and the Freemasons for years because of the inside edge the membership of certain groups gives their business. However, the way we're doing it has changed. Online business networks, such as Ecademy, are experiencing massive growth by using the internet to make business contacts both nationally and globally.

Face to face works

Don't try to network purely online, though. It's a good starting point, but you can't beat face-to-face events and looking into the whites of somebody's eyes for building relationships. There are local business communities in every major town which give members the opportunity to make money on their doorstep.

Another important use of networking is self-protection. With so many white collar jobs under threat due to outsourcing to lower-cost economies, it can be a case of network or starve. Networks can also provide some of the pastoral care and support no longer offered by employers.

But far too often, people only start networking at a point of crisis – when business is down or redundancy strikes – and then they make a complete nuisance of themselves. The point is to make contacts before you need them.

Networking might strike you as very un-British or even rude – going up to strangers and asking for something – but its advantages far outweigh any negatives. And it's a fun way to expand your social life, as well as your business circles.

So what are the secrets of building a great network?

Choose your targets

Networking is a strategic activity, which should be linked to specific business objectives. It needs to be carefully planned and executed. Ask yourself who you want to meet and why.

Are you trying to raise your visibility in a particular industry? If you are, who do you need to know? Are you hoping to find a new trading partner to promote your products and, if so, then who should you be considering? If you can't answer these questions, then you shouldn't be let out of the door.

Choose the right events

Once you've drawn up your hit list, just where do you meet them? Is it at the Institute of Directors (IoD), the top members organisation for senior business chiefs, or a local networking event? Are there professional associations which you would like to belong to, but which are by invitation only? If so, where do you need to go in order to get invited?

Many people choose the wrong events to do their networking, or never move beyond the obvious, such as Chamber of Commerce meetings. It's vital that you belong to several networks in order to develop both a breadth and depth of contacts.

It's also important to join the type of network that best fits your objectives and personality. Networks can be divided into 'soft contact networks', which are primarily social, and 'hard contact networks', which are much more sales-oriented. Soft contact networks, like Ecademy or Six Degrees, usually meet in the evening and may include a speaker, but the focus is on a drink and a chat. As these networks have less restricted membership, they can produce a wider range of contacts. But you may well have to kiss a lot of frogs to find your prince.

Hard contact networks, like BNI (www.bni-europe.com) or BRX (www.brxnet.co.uk), usually meet over breakfast, but membership at each branch is typically limited to one company per profession or industry. Members are asked to make formal company pitches to introduce themselves and to make referrals at each meeting. This can be an efficient way of networking if your time is limited and sales are what you're after, but your range of contacts may be more restricted.

Do your homework

Knowing who you want to meet beforehand means you can find out more about their company and interests. One of the benefits of online networking is that you can see who's going to be there beforehand and print off their profiles. It should be possible to obtain a list of exhibitors for any type of networking event, including trade fairs and exhibitions, so always study this information before the event itself.

Good networkers will always try to find common ground with those they're interested in meeting. Knowing what you share makes you relevant to the person you want to meet. It's daunting to go into a room with several hundred strangers, but if you've done your homework, it's much easier. And knowing something about who you want to talk to provides a useful starting point for conversation.

Get stuck in

Don't be afraid of approaching people, but don't waste their time or yours. Avoid talking about yourself. Instead find out what they do, and decide whether they could offer you some kind of opportunity. Also don't be afraid to move on, politely of course, as soon as you realise there's nothing in it for you.

Know how to get the conversation going

When you enter a room full of people, simply select the group of people you wish to join, say hello and ask to join them. Unless you luck upon a particularly obnoxious group, no one will ever say no, but it's important that you approach everyone you meet as a person first – not a sales prospect.

You could start by saying, 'I see you're interested in. . .' or mention the name of a contact you have in common. And there's nothing like a buffet line to start up a conversation about the food. But if you're attending a high-powered networking event, with key individuals you want to meet, you'll need to have more of a conversational strategy in order to succeed.

Having a memorised pitch in advance will make you sound rigid and uninspiring, but having a list of mental bullet points about what you do, your relevance to the other person and what you want to achieve is helpful. After using an opening that unites you, you can follow up with an introduction about yourself and what you do. Then you have to let people know what you're after and try to secure it. Whatever you propose should be of mutual benefit – and don't let your pitch close the conversation. You don't want people feeling that they have to get away from a salesperson.

Perfect pitch

One of the best business networking tips you can have is to be able to easily and succinctly describe what you do in less than 20 seconds. If you start with 'it's quite complicated...' you are going wrong.

It's not size that counts

You can't speak to everyone in the room. A realistic target is to make five or six good contacts per event. How many contacts you have in your personal network is a matter of some debate. Too many and you may never be able to manage them, but too few and your network will lack real power. It's up to you to find the right balance of quality and quantity.

Use business cards wisely

Exchange business cards only if you really want to, not because you feel you have to. Giving out cards should be a natural outcome of a good conversation, requested and exchanged, rather than something to be thrown around like confetti.

Once you have got somebody's business card, try to write a note to that person as soon as possible. Try to include something personal they mentioned, such as a birthday, hobby or something they're working on. This will make it easier for you to remember the person and to give you an opening next time you contact them.

And it's better to give business cards out to a few people you've talked to in more detail, who are more likely to remember you, than to scores of people you've chatted to only briefly.

Even though they're often overused, business cards remain an important networking tool. They provide important contact details. They help to remind you who you've met. And you'll need them to stay in touch.

Remember to ensure that you have enough to give out and that the contact details are up to date. You'd be surprised how many people have out-of-date business cards.

Be positive

There are three types of networkers: the apathetic; aggressive and positive. Apathetic networkers usually show, from their facial expression or body language, that they don't really want to be there – so it's no surprise that no one wants to talk to them. Aggressive 'spammers' are forever trying to hard-sell their product, which is an even bigger turn-off. But positive people – who are open, relaxed and smiling – are invariably the ones who get noticed.

Learn to remember names and faces

Here's one technique which works: When introduced to someone simply ask their name and then repeat it back to them. As you do so visualise someone you know well who has the same name standing beside them. If they then tell you that their company is, for instance, a bakery, then visualise your friend holding a loaf of bread. Try this for every person and, at the end of the event, look through all of your collected business cards and see if you can match the names to the faces.

Body language

If you find you would like to move on and you see someone else you would like to talk to, touch them lightly on the arm as they walk past, using this as a prompt to end the conversation. To encourage someone to contribute to the conversation, stand at a 90 degree angle, so others will feel comfortable about joining the group.

Give as well as take

Nobody likes to be aggressively sold to, but people feel obliged to consider a proposition from someone who has helped them. Great business networkers are often generous people and look for ways to help those that they meet. You already know people, you have knowledge, so be generous and help people out – they won't forget.

Networking is a two-way street. Those who use networking to take what they can get may find it works once, but not again. You've got to keep a running total in your mind of how much you've asked your network for favours. It's no problem going into debt as long as you eventually go back into credit. But if you're constantly in the red, your network will lose patience with you. And if you're constantly in the black, you're being exploited.

Be an active listener

Good listening skills are crucial in effective networking. This is so you can identify what the other person needs, show you understand, and then offer to help them in the best possible way. The art of good conversation also involves skilled questioning. If you ask closed questions you won't get much out of the conversation.

Don't overstay your welcome

A few minutes with each person is the norm, so don't overstay your welcome or allow yourself to be bored by those you are talking to. Remember the purpose of the event is to make useful business contacts, not friends. Don't feel you are being rude by saying that you need to work the room.

Make sure you're remembered

People may forget what you do or say, but they'll never forget how you make them feel. Treating everyone you meet with respect is essential – even if they have no immediate value to you. They may later on.

Good networkers try to connect people. Being considered a good matchmaker is the ultimate accolade. It gains friends and builds trust. And if you've been helpful, people are more likely to remember to do business with you in the future, or to give you a glowing referral. But if you don't follow up your contacts, memories will fade, no matter how good your initial impression.

Always follow up

As soon as you've made a useful contact, you should be thinking about how to build the relationship. It's also where most people go wrong.

After any event, you should go through any business cards you've collected and send an email saying that you enjoyed meeting that person. It's a good idea to scribble any action points on the card, such as 'Send quote for job'. If you've promised something, make sure you do it.

If there's something that you are doing which you think might well be of some interest to your contact, let them know. Keeping your ears open for business news that's relevant to them, or forwarding interesting articles from the internet, are other good ways to stay in touch.

Go for the long term

Once you've got a good contact, it's important to keep them. You must continue to regularly keep in touch. It's not just about saying 'can we do any work for you?' but asking 'how are you?' and taking an interest in their career. You need to cherish them in order to build a close relationship.

Networks need constant maintenance and monitoring, as well as replenishing. You could do regular appraisals to spot any gaps. Networking is about opportunities, to learn, share or trade. It can broaden your experience as well as your social life. But it should be considered a means to an end, not an end in itself.

Exhibitions and conferences

Working from home can sometimes be an isolating experience. Every now and again it's good to break out of the home office and actually meet some people face to face. As scary as this may seem, after months of dealing with people on the end of a phone or by email, getting face-time with real people can actually be a great way of marketing.

Live events work on several levels. If you have a budget for events, you can exhibit at an event that brings together the kind of people you want to become your clients. There are thousands of targeted business exhibitions in the UK, from must-attend annual national events where everybody in a sector will be, to more regular regional events targeting businesses in a specific locality.

These can be very cost-effective and in some cases you may be able to share stand space with other small businesses. Some exhibition organisers even have initiatives where they provide free or very cheap space to start-ups in the hope that they will grow their business and become the bigger exhibitors of tomorrow.

Take the opportunity to network

If you can't afford to exhibit, then exhibitions provide a great place to network, both among exhibitors and the visitors to the show. Most exhibitions have networking as part of the design, with spaces within the exhibition hall where you can meet other visitors, as well as events where you can mix. These could include seminars, parties, drinks receptions and industry association shindigs.

Taking up one of the speaking slots at an exhibition or conference provides a solid gold opportunity to put yourself in front of an influential audience – or a bunch of dozing students, depending on your luck. Organisers will usually post a request for papers several months in advance of the event. Try and find out if there is a particular theme for the conference and adapt your presentation accordingly.

These slots are a way to promote your expertise, but they should be regarded as a soft sell. Thirty Powerpoint slides of personal advertising will simply have people heading for the door. Aim to deliver a presentation that addresses issues of importance to the industry and produces some insight for those assembled.

Include contact details on the final slide and offer the presentation to anybody who has attended the event. Networking after the session, remember to exchange cards and follow up on any requests for more information.

WANT TO KNOW MORE...

For more information on exhibitions, check out these websites:

- www.aeo.org.uk
- www.eventia.org.uk.

Getting the most out of an exhibition visit

- Plan ahead and set objectives for your visit. Why do you want to attend? What do you hope to achieve?
- Pre-register to save paying an entry fee on the day registration. This means you will receive pre-show news, offers and invitations to networking events.
- Review the exhibitor list before the exhibition. Time spent doing a little research will pay off. Prioritise your key areas of interest and review your list at least once in the day.
- Take advantage of free education and seminars. Don't be complacent. You may well learn something new.
- Use your time wisely. Remember that it is a working day, and not a jolly. Give yourself enough time to achieve what you want and don't try to cram in too much.
- Prepare a list of essential supplier companies to visit and include your key suppliers as well as new contacts.
- Manage your time, book appointments, plan your route around the maze of stands and make sure you keep to your time schedule.
- Come equipped with a notebook and pen, and a mini stapler to attach business cards to any documentation you collect.
- Use your smartphone to take pictures of QR codes and products.
- Network! Exhibitions are the ideal place to catch up with suppliers, clients and competitors and share new trends and ideas.
- Review the information and business cards gathered at the show and take the appropriate action: give them a call, set up a meeting, send more information, or drop them a quote.

Body language at networking events

- Keep moving: it's easy to freeze when you enter a room full of people you don't know. Keep moving and head straight up to somebody straight away. This will establish your routine for the rest of the meeting and will give you confidence that you have broken the ice.
- Be open: maintain an open posture to invite people to speak to you. Crossing your arms is a classic defensive sign and will keep people at arm's length.
- Clothes maketh the man: always dress professionally and smartly. If it suits you an eye-catching element, such as a colourful tie or unusual brooch, may help people to remember you.
- Punctuality: it always seems a lot easier to introduce yourself to someone when you are one of the first arrivals.
- Get introduced: ask hosts and organisers to introduce you to people. They are generally well connected and it's in their interest to do so.
- Listen actively: you don't have to be a great speaker to network well, but you must show people that they have your full attention. Maintain full eye contact with them while they speak and nod while you listen, pacing your nod to the rhythm of their speaking. Don't go mad, though – you don't want to start headbanging at them. Mirror their gestures as a way of building empathy. Don't look away or you will seem bored.
- Poker face: mouth movements can give away all sorts of clues. We purse our lips and sometimes twist them to the side when we're thinking. We might also do it to bite back an angry comment. Nevertheless, it will probably be spotted by other people and although they may not know the content of the comment, they will get a feeling you were not too pleased.
- Breaking into a group: this can seem a bit daunting, but if you move into the largest gap in the group and acknowledge the people in the group with a look and a smile, it is easier. Then use active listening signs to establish a place in the group, while waiting for a chance to make a contribution. When there is a gap, acknowledge what somebody else has just said and then introduce yourself quickly before beginning to speak.
- Make your excuses: if you can't find a way in, acknowledge somebody across the room with a wave and move off purposefully as if you have plenty of other fish to fry.

- Don't be a space invader: distance from others is crucial if you want to give off the right signals. Stand too close and you'll seem pushy or 'in your face'. Stand or sit too far away and you'll seem 'stand-offish'. You don't want to give either impression, so if you're in a group situation, observe how close the other people are to each other and take your cue from them. If you move closer to someone and they back away, you've probably overstepped the mark and should pull back a little.
- Be calm: don't fidget or play with things in your hands. Playing with a pen or tapping with your foot against the table is an annoying distraction.
- Smile: it puts everybody at their ease to have a smiling person in the group. Smiling makes you more approachable and enables you to have a more productive networking session. Practise your smile in a mirror so that you appear natural and not psychotic.

Networking online

Networking need no longer just be about drinking cheap white wine in hotel meeting rooms. There are a growing number of opportunities to network with freelancers all over the world. Social networking sites and online communication options are making geographical boundaries almost no barrier for establishing a network. So, how do you go about it?

Get active

Taking action is the first and most critical step to building a strong network. Online networking can be uncomfortable for some people at first, so start with whatever you feel comfortable with (blogging, forums, networking sites, social media, etc.). Practice makes perfect.

Focus your efforts

There are so many places and ways that you can network as a freelancer that you'll never be able to use all of them. Focus on quality over quantity. Rather than having a small involvement at many sites, build a strong presence at just a few.

Schedule it

Networking can be a low priority when you're busy. If you build some time for networking into your schedule, you'll find that the results are more than worth the time. Once you've chosen one or more sites to actively use, set aside some time for building your presence, responding to emails and commenting on blogs.

Have a base

As you start to build your network online, it is necessary to have somewhere to point people towards. You may use other networking sites and most of them will give you the opportunity to link back to your own website or blog. By having a blog you'll be able to interact with other freelancers and your blog posts will draw others to your site and open up the lines of communication. Make sure that your blog allows people to contact you and encourage them to do so.

Respect your contacts

Networking online can seem less personal than meeting face to face, but you must treat online connections with respect and as having equal value to those offline.

Building a network on LinkedIn

LinkedIn is one of the fastest growing ways to network online. Here are a few tips on how to make it work for you. (For information on using LinkedIn as a marketing tool, see the business tips on pp 130–131.)

Complete your profile

Don't be modest. Include the most impressive parts of your CV in the appropriate fields. Think of the profile as an ad for your freelance skills. Use active verbs like 'led', 'developed', 'produced' and 'sold' to sell yourself.

Include keywords that a potential client might be searching for. Look at the profiles of other freelancers in your field for inspiration.

Claim your LinkedIn name

Click on Profile and then scroll down to where it says Public Profile. Click Edit to change from a random string of characters to your name. This means people can search for your first and last name. If the name has been taken, try reversing the order of first and last names. If that's already in use, you could insert a middle initial or even use a nickname.

Building your network

LinkedIn will search your email account for people you may want to connect with. You can also manually enter email addresses or search for specific people. It's best only to connect with people you know and trust. Remember that you are judged by the company you keep. Search for contacts you'd like to network with and add them to your network.

Unless you've done business, add them as a friend. Include a message introducing yourself, and explaining how you found them (LinkedIn will show how connected they are to you). Spell out how it might be beneficial for you both to be part of the same network.

Recommendations

Try to get others to sing your praises. Scroll down to the Experience section and click 'Request Recommendations'. Don't carpet bomb people, but rather try and target those people who you think will have good things to say about you.

Be available

If you have disabled the contact requests option, you are restricting your ability to expand your network.

Display your email address

People cannot find you through your email address if you have not either left it within your summary or within your contact details on LinkedIn. Make sure it is made public.

Promote your LinkedIn page

Include it in your email signature and your blog or website. Facebook has an app that enables you to place a LinkedIn button within your profile.

Update your status

Use tools like TweetDeck and Ping that allow you to post updates to multiple platforms at the same time.

Join groups

Joining groups or starting one of your own that is related to your industry is a good networking tool. Invite members from LinkedIn and elsewhere, and provide content to it on a regular basis. With good content, your group will increase in size, and it will provide a good platform to engage with your networks, promote your sites and work in a professional environment.

Awards

This may seem an odd way to try to promote your business, but awards can boost your profile and morale overnight and provide a great source of validation that you are doing something right. They have even spawned an industry dedicated to helping businesses make their applications more likely to win.

There are hundreds, if not thousands, of business awards given every year, some of which come with a financial or support package as a prize, as well as a nice trophy to show your mum.

Awards are given out by a range of organisations, from government agencies to private companies. Each award will have its own specific entry requirements and criteria, but in virtually all cases businesses must show why they should be rewarded for their work over the past year. These could be worthy for a number of reasons, such as launching a product or overcoming setbacks and difficulties.

In some cases you can nominate yourself, while in others you may have to be nominated by somebody else. Most are free to enter and require only a little application. This may give you a great story to take to the press and a great addition to your CV.

The following are all awards entry consultants and include lists and databases of awards:

→ www.awards-agency.co.uk

→ www.awardsintelligence.co.uk

→ www.boost-marketing.co.uk.

Startups Tip

You can also try entering the Startups awards, which recognise the UK's most creative, innovative and ambitious new businesses, Visit www.startups.co.uk/startups-awards.

Pitching for work

Unless you are very lucky, work will not simply roll in. At some point in time you are going to have to get out there and hustle for it. You will also want to vary the type of work that you get and expand the portfolio of clients you work for. Remember that it is risky to put all of your eggs in one basket by being over-reliant on one source of employment.

Try to dedicate a set amount of time each week to trying to find new work. Devise a system for pitching that works for you. Nobody likes cold calling or following up emails, but unless you pester people, the chances are they are not going to get back to you.

Cold calling can lead directly to work, or it can give you a foot in the door to be considered for future jobs. You could send an email, but a targeted phone call can put you straight through to someone who can deal with you there and then. It's also an opportunity to start building a relationship with somebody and get on their radar, rather than simply being an anonymous emailer.

Even if you have done your homework, it can be difficult to get a pitch right first time round. Reading up on a company will give you an idea of the type of work they are after, but without some context, you may be wide of the mark in terms of detail. For example, a freelance journalist must know about style, deadlines, what work is commissioned to freelancers and what is written by in-house journalists, what they have covered before, and what is on the editorial schedule going forward.

There are two kinds of pitching.

1.   Pitching specific ideas to a client, e.g. a freelance writer suggesting ideas to a magazine.

2.   Pitching yourself as a prospective freelance supplier, e.g. a freelance designer looking to get on somebody's roster.

The kind of business you are in will determine which pitch you need to make. In some cases, you may be pitching both your ideas and yourself.

Ideas and experience

When you have a good picture of the kind of work that a client wants, put together a list of ideas that they might be interested in. Try to avoid the obvious and come up with original ideas or give a twist to old favourites. The people who work for the company will have their own ideas, so they'll have already thought of obvious ones. You have to prove your value by giving them something different.

At other times, pitching is about emphasising your experience and credentials. The important thing is to make sure that your pitch fits the needs of the company you are pitching to. For this reason, there is no one size fits all pitch. You should carefully tailor the way you pitch to the needs of each company. Any commissioner will want to be satisfied that you understand their business and that you have come to them with a reasoned pitch that aims to serve those needs.

Be persistent

If you do get knocked back, don't think that the idea was a bad one. It may simply be a case of right idea, wrong client or the wrong time.

Have backup clients in mind. You could even approach them all simultaneously and see who bites first.

There will also be times when a client gets straight back to you because they want the work now! Be sure that when you pitch an idea you are prepared for this eventuality. Do you know who you will need to contact or work with to complete the work? Have you done some background research? Does the idea actually hold water in the first place? Do you have time to turn it around on a tight deadline?

If your pitch is more about you as a potential supplier, the rules about doing your homework in advance are pretty much the same. Thereafter you are looking to get a foot in the door to convince the company that you can do a job for them.

> **Startups Tip**
> Create a list of companies that could use your services. Try to address your enquiries towards a named individual.

Cold calls

You may not be a salesperson, but learning the art of cold calling is important if you are to be a successful freelancer. Here are some tips on how to do it.

→ Do some research to build a list of companies that use freelancers and that you can pitch to. Check your contacts book for any contacts you can revisit, and augment this with names from websites, trade association memberships, directories, lists of delegates from conferences you have attended, companies mentioned in the media, and any other leads you come across.

→ Try to get the name of somebody that you can speak to, rather than asking for 'the person who commissions freelancers' or something that sounds like a phishing expedition.

→ Be prepared to be knocked back, have the phone slammed down on you, and for people to be generally shirty with you. It's not usually personal – think how you feel when your workflow is interrupted by a sales call.

→ Devise a script for your calls. This may seem a little robotic, but it allows you to focus on the message you are trying to get across and will help you be succinct and to the point.

→ Introduce yourself and provide a quick reason behind your call: 'Good morning. My name is Joe Bloggs and I'm a freelance designer. I'm calling to find out if I can help with your web or graphic design needs.'

→ Leave this message on the voicemail system, with your contact number if no one is available to speak to directly.

→ Be professional and courteous in your calls. Don't try to be too pushy, and try to read the mood of the individual you are speaking to in order to get the most from the call.

→ In most cases, the answer will be no, but if people want more information you can then go on to provide it, such as details of the kinds of services you offer and projects you have worked on, as well as dealing with any specific queries.

→ Make a record of the response to your calls: was it a flat 'no thank you'? Was more information required? Does the company want you to contact them in future?

→ Drop an email to anybody who has expressed any level of interest, reiterating what you can do for them and including your contact details, plus your blog and Twitter address.

→ Remember that cold calling is a numbers game, so set aside a decent time period each week to get your calls in.

→ Follow up warm leads regularly, as well as contacting clients that have given you work in the past. Keep your files on the companies updated with any information you have gleaned about upcoming projects and potential jobs.

How to get commissioned

Picking up regular freelance commissions is the essence of making a successful freelance career. You need to be pitching ideas and then getting work from your pitches continuously. Some freelancers will supplement this by having ongoing commitments such as shifts where they are working in a client's office.

Contacts are the most important thing to ensure a healthy flow of work. You need to make contact with people senior enough to look at your ideas and skills, but also to give you the green light to do the work. For this reason, nurturing the right contacts is important. You may find that you get on great with a reporter that you've met on a press trip, but that they may have little sway when it comes to commissioning.

Who has the clout?

Getting to know the people who matter and what they are looking for from freelancers is crucial. This can be time consuming and involves a lot of work for you in assessing the kind of work that a commissioner is after, and getting front of mind with them. Ultimately you want them to be picking up the phone to you and offering you work. This is a lot easier than coming up with lots of creative ideas and pitching them individually to the commissioner. Researching and pitching ideas takes time, and if none of them are used, it's dead time financially.

However, to get to get to this point, you need to prove your worth, which is where all your pitching skills come into play.

Remember that getting commissioned is an important part of the freelance life, so always be alert to opportunities to get commissioned. Don't leave the search for work until you have none. Take the opportunities presented every day to fire off a few speculative story ideas to potential clients. Or simply use the time to forge a better relationship with the contacts that you have.

Call back

Timing is everything in commissioning. A commissioner wants their life to be made as easy as possible. Sometimes a friendly email or phone call will be enough to nudge the latest commission in your direction; if your interjection reminds them that you are around, still freelancing (people disappear from the freelance pool all the time, either back to full-time jobs, new areas completely, or they retire) and full of enthusiasm, then work will come your way.

Work on your elevator pitch technique. Try to hone your pitch down to a couple of quick and easy-to-understand sentences that will give the commissioner a good idea of what you are proposing. Detail is unimportant at this stage. If it fires their imagination you can fill in the blanks at a later date. If it leaves them cold, then you haven't wasted much of their, or your, time.

Creating and using an elevator pitch

Being a freelancer is a bit like being a Boy Scout, in that you should always 'Be Prepared'. In this instance, you need to be prepared to unleash your sales pitch on individuals who could become clients.

Often freelancers will simply say 'I'm a freelance web designer' when asked what they do, or talk about individual projects. The problem with this approach is that it can close off the possibility of selling yourself and your skills.

Your elevator pitch should almost be like your boiler plate statement. It's a brief advertisement about what you do. The idea is that if you were in an elevator with someone who asked what you did, you could convey the most important details of your business before the ride had finished.

Of course, not many of us have those sorts of conversations in lifts. More often they are a place for embarrassed silences and gazing at feet. But we do meet people all the time in other circumstances where there are business opportunities, such as networking events, conferences, product launches and press events, so it's important to create an elevator pitch that intrigues the listener, creates awareness of what you do, and leaves them wanting to know more and stay in touch.

A successful pitch needs to cover the three questions all businesses initially have to answer.

1. Who you are.

2. What you do.

3. Why customers should care.

It's a good idea to write your pitch down. The description needs to spell out what you do specifically, but in a succinct manner. Treat it as if you were making a list of the three or four most important things you do for someone who has no idea about your job.

Practise until pitch perfect.

On a separate list, write the three main reasons why a client should hire you rather than someone else. This can include your specialties, your experience, your training, or any other plus points. The two lists can be combined to make your elevator pitch.

Although you don't need to memorise the words like a robot, it's a good idea to practise so that it becomes second nature to you. Time yourself to see if you can get it under the magic 30 seconds (and have a longer version for slower elevators). Try it out on some friends to see what they think. You could even tape yourself to hear what it sounds like. Play about with it until it is something that you are happy with and that sounds like it really represents you.

The next step is to actually use your pitch. Rather than opt for small talk at business events, try and work your pitch into conversations. Always be ready to expand on what you do, and have business cards ready to distribute to anybody who looks like a good business opportunity.

Accepting commissions

When you are offered a commission, always make sure that you are clear about what it involves. It is a good idea to see a written brief before you accept a piece of work. Sometimes a phone call will make a job sound irresistible, but you will find out at a later date that it has some awkward aspects to it, such as a tight deadline that doesn't fit your schedule, a requirement to travel, or covers an area where you feel you lack expertise.

Take some time before accepting a contract. If you have had a phone conversation with a commissioning person and everything sounds okay, then tell them it shouldn't be a problem, but that you would like to see the brief first.

Before taking on any piece of work, you need to establish a few things.

→ Who is offering you the work, and what is their position within the commissioning organisation?

→ What are you expected to do? What are the precise details of the brief, such as the deadline and the form that the work must be submitted in, and what rights does the commission cover (e.g. all rights, first publication rights, online rights etc)?

→ Who is your contact for any issues that arise while you are carrying out the commission?

→ What are the conditions and rates of pay that you are accepting? Preferably, get this in writing.

→ When can you expect to be paid, and in what form, i.e. cheque or BACS? Will the payment be staggered in any way?

→ Will expenses be paid for any out of pocket payments you may have to make, such as parking or travel?

→ Get the commissioning brief in writing. Although an oral brief is as much a contract as a written one, it is much harder to prove what has been agreed if any issues arise.

→ If a written brief doesn't appear, write your own brief and submit it to the commissioning person to see if they agree with what has been agreed. It's better to be safe than sorry.

→ If a commissioner catches you unprepared, or you need to think about what the job entails, break off negotiations so that you can work out a reasonable fee before continuing the discussion.

Kill fees

Kill fees are not as deadly as they sound, although they won't do your bank balance any good.

A kill fee is what happens in publishing when an editor changes their mind about a piece. They may decide not to run it for a range of reasons, such as the magazine size shrinking, a competitor running a similar feature, or a change of direction in the magazine. The kill fee is a payment given to the freelancers in exchange for not running the piece. It is typically half the agreed fee, although in some cases a lower amount may be offered.

The NUJ recommends that any work commissioned and delivered on time and to specification should be paid for in full, whatever happens to it after that.

However, it is up to the individual freelancer to decide whether to press the issue. If the client provides a fair bit of work, then discretion may be the better part of valour and you should accept their offer.

Be prepared to negotiate calmly and reasonably with them, and do not feel that you have to accept their offer without doing so.

In the best circumstances, you may be offered a kill fee before you have started work on a project. But don't count on that happening too often.

Checklist

☑ Assess where your work is likely to come from and use this as the basis for marketing yourself.

☑ Decide how you will market yourself to potential employers. What are your strengths? What can you add to their business? What marketing channels will you use to communicate with them?

☑ Is your website content optimised for search engines? Use Google Keyword Tools to research keywords for your site, and ensure you update the content regularly.

☑ Identify which social media platforms your customers will be using – Facebook, Twitter, LinkedIn, YouTube? As you start to operate across a number of social media platforms, you can use a product such as Tweetdeck or Hootsuite to manage your social media output.

☑ Use Google Analytics to track and measure social media conversions.

☑ Create a list of potential customers and try to dedicate a set amount of time each week to finding new work.

☑ Look to pitch original ideas at the people who can provide you with work. Work on perfecting your elevator pitch.

CHAPTER 6

Succeeding in your freelance career

📖 What's in this chapter?

Now that you've mastered the art of pitching your work and getting commissioned, you need to focus on making your freelance career a success. This starts with knowing what to charge for your work and extends to learning how to manage your time so you can fulfil all of your commissions and become known as a reliable supplier. Once you've mastered these things you may even find that you have enough work to look at hiring someone else. In this chapter we'll look at:

→ how to price your work

→ how to manage your time

→ how to become a reliable supplier

→ the key to getting repeat work

→ what you need to do if you decide you want to turn freelancing into a business.

Pricing your work

Knowing what to charge for your work can be quite an awkward area for the new freelancer. Up until now you have not had to think too much about the value of what you do. You just turned up at work, did the hours and got a fat (or not so fat) pay cheque at the end of the month. Your employer was the one who knew the price to charge for services, and how much your contribution was worth to them.

Now *you* are in that situation. People will often call freelancers up and ask 'what are your rates?' It's a straightforward enough question, but the answer is not actually that simple. Many freelancers will charge different rates for different jobs for the simple reason that not all jobs are the same.

→ Some jobs are more demanding of your time and experience than others.

→ Some jobs have a shorter deadline.

→ Some jobs require you to work unsociable hours or in a different location.

→ Some freelancers have different rate for different types of client. For instance, they may charge a lower rate to a charity or a not for profit organisation. They may accept less working for an organisation that is interesting to work for, or whose project will look good in their portfolio.

→ Some jobs have higher costs involved.

For these and other reasons, it can be hard to have a set rate. However, clients will often need a ball park figure, so you should do some research into how much you are going to charge and what the market can bear.

The going rate

Generally, clients will want to be quoted on a day rate or in the case of something like photography, a half-day rate. However, for some smaller jobs, such as a PR person writing up a press release, you may be asked to quote by the hour. Some freelancers don't like taking on too many hourly paid jobs, as they can be difficult to schedule and may rule out other work for the rest of the day.

If you are charging by the hour, take your hourly rate and multiply by the number of hours dedicated to the project. Then add in any expenses, like travel or stationery, and send the invoice to your client. Keep a record of the hours worked on a worksheet to ensure there are no misunderstandings.

If a project is for a longer period, you may be willing to offer a slightly lower rate to seal the deal. This may allow you to negotiate other benefits, such as working flexitime, as part of a trade-off.

Start by asking some friendly freelancers what they charge and what the going rate in the market is. Try to speak to some clients and find out what they pay. Your old company might be a good place to start. Recruitment agencies that place temporary staff can also give you a steer on what the going rate is and some agency websites include a guide to current freelance rates. However bear in mind that agencies take a commission on placements so their rates may be lower than what you would get working directly for a client.

See Chapter 1 (pp 13–14) for some real rates from freelance members.

Keep an eye on what full-time staff are being paid for equivalent jobs by looking at online ads in publications and websites such as the *Guardian*, *Marketing* and *PR Week*. This can help you work out what companies will pay freelancers. Generally, the daily or weekly rate should be higher, to make up for the flexibility of the freelancer resource and the fact that employers don't have to pay National Insurance, holidays or benefits.

Setting your rates

When you start out you should charge around the market rate. However, be flexible. If you don't have a great deal of experience, you may find more work comes your way if you charge a slightly lower rate. Be careful you don't set your rates too low, though, as it will be difficult to raise them at a later date. Also, bear in mind that nobody will use you just because you are cheap if the quality of the work isn't there. So you will be expected to deliver the same standard of work as somebody who is charging more.

It's a delicate balancing act, but don't undervalue what you do. You have to be able to make a living, but you don't want to price yourself out of the equation. The size of the client is relevant, as smaller companies may pay less than large corporations. Location will be a factor, with London paying higher rates than elsewhere in the country.

Your level of expertise will also affect what you can charge. If you have attained a certain level in your field, then clients are paying for that ability and the fact that you can be expected to take on more involved tasks.

Negotiating

Clients have a budget for a job, but they won't necessarily tell you what it is. If they ask you what your rates are, then they are effectively looking to start negotiating with you.

If possible, always ask the client what they are offering in the first place. Getting them to put their offer on the table puts you in a stronger bargaining position. There is an element of bluff about all negotiations, so be prepared to be quite bullish about what you want. It is easier to start with a (perhaps unrealistically) high figure and then negotiate down. Hardly anybody will be able to negotiate upwards. If a client accepts your quoted rate then the chances are that they were prepared to pay more for the job.

How to make your case

You don't have to be aggressive in negotiations. Often a few moments of friendly discussion can leave you meeting in the middle. Nobody likes to feel that they have been 'had' in negotiations, so the best way to present your case is by stressing the value that you provide through valid business arguments, such as:

→ you are an expert in your field and you are known for the quality of your work

→ the client's rates have not risen for some time, and may be behind their competitors

→ you have added value to a job in some way.

Although your rates can be flexible, you will want to gradually increase your rates. Nobody will willingly give you a pay rise as a freelancer and the rates that clients pay can be stubbornly static. At the same time, your costs will be rising year on year. If you are constantly busy and people are happy with your work, then the time could be right to raise your rates.

It is tough to raise your rates with an existing client who will probably claim that their budgets are set and that they don't have any wriggle room at the minute. You need to present the reasons behind your rate rise in a business-like manner and not simply as a fait accompli. Explain the service you offer, the benefits of using your services and why you provide a better service than your competitors.

One area that you should be wary of is the type of job board that adopts an auction approach. Generally these sites are populated by people looking for the lowest cost, so try not to get dragged down to the lowest common denominator.

Some projects will require you to charge by the hour, whereas others will be charged on a project basis. When you are taking on work that is by the hour, make sure that the hourly rate is at a premium to your usual daily rate; otherwise, you are simply encouraging people to take slithers of your time. This makes managing your time difficult and you should be pushing them towards using you for a whole day if possible.

Quoting for a job

Where you are asked to price up a long-term project, assess it carefully in advance.

→ What does the project involve?

↝ Who is the client (and what can they afford to pay)?

↝ What is your involvement, e.g. are you central to making it happen, or do you have a more junior role?

↝ How can you measure results?

↝ How will the project end?

↝ What is the value of the project to the client?

↝ What skills are you delivering to the project?

Your quote will be based on your assessment of the complexity of the task, the time it will take and your rate.

There are also times when it becomes a case of 'knowing where to hit', when the job does not take long, but you are paid because you have very specific skills that the client needs. Think of this like the engineer who comes to fix your immobile car, bangs the engine with a spanner and gets it working again. You pay him for the end result, not the time he has spent fixing your car.

Present your proposal to your client and sell your service on the price. Emphasise the benefits of your service to the client and what they are getting from you. You can break down each part of a project if you think that the client needs that level of transparency, but don't undervalue what you offer.

Don't be afraid to explain why you charge what you do. Your fees cover all of your costs and must reflect what you need to charge to remain in business. Some freelancers, such as photographers, can have very high overheads that they need to pass on to clients. They should also expect to pay more for unusual requests, exclusive material, or tight deadlines.

Make sure you are clear about what a project entails. If you have any questions, submit them in writing and get them to write down their answers to your questions. A brief that everybody is happy with is essential to concluding a project satisfactorily. After all, this is what will lead to more work in future.

How to calculate an hourly rate

Your rates should reflect what it costs you to be in business. Anyone selling time and knowledge as a service can calculate their costs.

The first step is to determine your costs – what it will cost you to be in, and run, the business.

Don't underestimate the full costs of starting up and maintaining a business. Remember to include all your costs, including ongoing expenses and fresh investments in equipment.

Your main costs are:

→ business and office expenses

→ salary and tax

→ benefits.

Business and office expenses

You'll need an office, even if it's in your home (see Chapter 4 for more information on the costs of setting up a home office). Ongoing recurring expenses will include phone and utility bills, postage, broadband and web hosting, copying, office supplies, memberships, subscriptions, travel and professional services such as accountancy.

You will also have to invest in office equipment and furniture, computer purchases and upgrades, filing cabinets, a desk and so on.

Salary and tax

Plan to earn more or less what you'd get as a full-time employee, otherwise being an employee may be less stressful.

Don't forget that you are now responsible for your own tax affairs and you must put a relevant sum aside from your income. It is a good idea to open a separate account for your tax. With online banking this is very simple, and you can put aside the money in an interest bearing account of some type. This way, even though the taxman is getting their slice, you are making the money work for you while it's resting in your account.

Benefits

This could include such items as pension, insurance and holiday pay that you will now have to fund.

By adding these three items together you will arrive at a figure that represents your cost of being in business for the year.

Next, calculate your billable time. First, work out how many hours you will be able to work.

This needs to take account of all the down time that you will not be able to charge for:

→ holidays

→ sick days off

→ time without work

→ unpaid work time such as personal admin or marketing.

Try to come up with a realistic number of hours you can expect to charge for, for example 1,500 hours across the year.

Divide your total cost for the year by the number of hours to come up with an hourly rate.

With this hourly rate, you can calculate a daily and weekly rate. It is worth asking around to see if this is realistic. If the consensus is that you are being a bit optimistic, you will either have to revisit your salary expectations, look at ways of cutting costs, or think again about the type of work you are pursuing. If your hourly rate seems too low then raise it until you feel comfortable with it.

If you are surprisingly popular and never seem to be without work, it could be time to rethink your hourly rate. On the other hand, if clients are put off by your hourly rate, then you could consider lowering it.

Freelancing is a marathon, not a sprint, and sometimes it can pay off to play the long game and accept a lower rate in the hope of future benefit: for example, if you think a client will be a good source of work in future, or a project will give you valuable experience.

Time management

Many freelancers complain that 24 hours are just not enough in a day. It is a frequent cry when you are responsible for doing everything, as you are in a one-man band. There is nobody else to turn to when things get busy, so to be successful as a freelancer you have to get super organised, and that means making the best use of your time.

When starting out, you will almost definitely be at your desk late into the night, early in the mornings and throughout the weekend.

The question is, can you operate effectively at such a pace for long? It seems like common sense that people do not work effectively when constantly flat-out. We can all put in all-nighters every now and then, when sheer adrenalin will keep us going to the end of a project, but in the longer term it doesn't work.

Unfortunately, one of the plusses of freelancing – that you can be flexible with your hours – is also a downside. It is not generally a 9 to 5 existence, and it is easy to find yourself working outside of these times. Then you also have the administration to deal with, often during the evenings or at weekends.

The increasingly global nature of business, particularly for anyone running a website as part of their business, also means that working hours are extending – a work phone call at 9pm or even 4am is not unusual for website owners.

It can be hard to turn down work as a freelancer. Even if you are manically busy, it is impossible to say no because of the fear that all existing work will dry up and that you will be left with nothing.

However, if deadlines are missed, clients lose faith. However good the work, it is of little use when the deadline has passed. Clients are also quick to point out this failing to others and may recommend you but with a warning about your timekeeping.

The key to make it all work is time management. However, you have to find the right solution to suit you and your personality. It is no good suggesting that you tidy your desk daily if you are a person who hates tidying. You will resent the effort and soon stop making it. But there will be another solution for you.

Few people go freelance in order to spend time on administration and all the other chores that come with it. For the sake of sanity, it is worth applying a few time management techniques to reduce time spent on those things and free up hours to spend on the work that sets you apart.

Make lists

It may seem slightly anal to start the day making a list, but a few minutes doing so can keep you focused on what you need to achieve during the working day. You also gain a great deal of satisfaction from achieving listed goals and being able to cross things off a list.

Keeping track of your schedule is hugely important. It is all too easy to forget to send an invoice as one job is completed and you dive headlong towards the next deadline. Making lists is a top tip because it helps organise the tasks in your head and helps prioritise the tasks ahead.

Make sure that conversations with clients are logged in your diary and that agreed actions are noted somewhere prominent so that those actions do actually go forward.

A page-a-day diary is useful for just this purpose, allowing you to record what you need to do and have done hour by hour. Keep this diary up to date, filling it in as you speak to clients.

It doesn't really matter where you keep your list; you could use a computer, Post-It notes, or your diary. It's an aide-memoire to keep you focused. Just make sure you don't spend more time making your list than doing the things on it.

How to make a to-do list

A written to-do list is a simple technique that can increase your productivity by 20% or more. It also has extra benefits such as clearing your mind and saving you energy and stress.

Spend five to 10 minutes each day planning your activities with a daily to-do list. You could even produce your plan at the end of the previous day, but it is important that you actually write down your tasks.

After you've listed all your tasks, review your to-do list and decide on the priority of each task. Give higher priority to the tasks that get you closer to your goals.

Rate the tasks A, B or C, where:

⇢ A tasks are critical to your goals and must be done that day

⇢ B tasks are less urgent but still important. You can start them once the A tasks are done

⇢ C tasks are nice to do but can safely be left until another day.

If a new unplanned task comes in during the day, take time to assess its priority, as it may affect how the rest of your day shapes up.

Try to break complex tasks into smaller manageable pieces that you can do one at a time. It will give you a greater sense of achievement as you cross them off during the day.

Plan your time

Time is a finite resource, so look carefully at what you want to achieve with your time and plan accordingly. Forward planning will allow you to allocate the right time to jobs and employ the relevant resources to achieve deadlines.

Try to get some rhythm into your working life. We love working in patterns, so if we can start implementing tasks that recur at regular intervals during the week, our brains will quickly snap into the right mode.

Freelancers have a set number of tasks to complete each week, such as marketing, sales, accounting or business development. By defining these key tasks and working out when we will do them, we stay focused.

Try not to stray from this schedule. If you get marketing ideas, write them down and keep them for your marketing time. Doing this will allow you to think about those ideas a little further before rushing into them.

Creating a weekly calendar will help. This might seem a bit like being back at school – oh no, double admin on Wednesday afternoon – but it ensures that you allocate an appropriate time to the functions that are important for your freelance career.

Prioritise

All jobs are important, but some jobs are more important than others. Knowing which are which is essential to good time management. Priorities for a freelancer should be tasks that contribute directly to you getting paid. However, other people's priorities can be completely different – for example, your accountant wanted you to file the paperwork for your accounts a month ago. Everything is important eventually, but prioritisation is about deciding what absolutely has to be done today.

Consider other people. Are they waiting on you to finish something to allow them to continue with their jobs? If so, then you will have to move that item up the list. What are the consequences of failing to do something? If you will lose a client over it, then it is a major priority.

Constantly re-evaluate what's on your to-do list. Priorities change, so don't simply continue working to a list that has been superseded by actual events.

Use technology

Make life easier for yourself by letting technology take the strain. Something as simple as an online calendar with a system of reminders can make an enormous difference to your productivity. There are lots of online list services, such as Vitalist (www.vitalist.com) or Remember the Milk (www.rememberthemilk.com), which you can use to help you stay on top of your workload.

For more complex tasks, you can use project management software, such as Basecamp (http://basecamp.com) or Backpack (http://backpackit.com). These are particularly useful if you are collaborating with others on a project, as they allow you to share information and store notes on how a project is progressing.

Contact management tools, such as Big Contacts (www.bigcontacts.com) or Highrise (http://highrisehq.com), can be helpful for freelancers that need to maintain close contact with their clients. They allow you to access call information, details of meetings and actions that have to be concluded.

Group tasks

One of the difficult things about freelancing is that there are many things pulling you in different directions during the day. Grouping together similar items allows you to do them at the same time. Rather than disrupting your concentration by responding to emails the moment they arrive, why not set aside time each day to respond to all client emails at once? Set aside time to deal with invoicing once or twice per week.

Small, easily achieved tasks can also be grouped together and tackled at once.

Don't be distracted

It's easy to kid yourself that something is a priority, but as a freelancer you have to be honest about what is important and what you shouldn't be wasting your time on. Easier and more pleasant tasks can float to the top of the to-do list, even though they don't deserve to be there.

If you work from home, don't get dragged into events in the rest of the house. Emphasise to your family that your office is out of bounds during the day as a way of preventing your focus from drifting. Similarly, don't allow yourself to drift into the front room to check out the latest soap opera during your coffee break. Your five minute break can quickly become half an hour of wasted time.

Delegate what others can do more effectively

Although the temptation as a freelancer is to do everything yourself, to keep costs down, it is sometimes a false economy. Accounts are the obvious example here. It may take you a few days to do something that an accountant or bookkeeper could sort out in half a day. Your time is too valuable to be wasting it doing tasks that others are better trained for.

Just say no

It's hard to turn down work, but on occasion it makes sense to do so. Too much work can be as bad as too little if you end up pushing yourself and quality lapses as a result. Be realistic about how long a job will take and where your existing deadlines lie before taking something on. It will do you more good in the long run if you politely decline work due to being too busy. It can even make you more desirable in the future if a client sees how in demand you are. Remember to suggest another reliable freelancer who may be able to take on the work in your stead, and let the freelancer know where the referral came from so they can return the favour in future if they are able.

Take time out

Regular breaks during the day will help you maintain concentration. A five to 10 minute screen break every hour is recommended for anybody working with a computer monitor. As well as giving your eyes a rest from the glare, a break will allow you to mentally recharge your batteries and come back to a task refreshed. Don't spend the time watching TV, but do something that genuinely helps you refresh, such as taking a walk, making a cuppa or even closing your eyes for a few minutes.

> **Startups Tip**
> Changing the task you are working on, rather than sticking to the same job all day, can also refresh you.

Don't forget your holidays

Nobody will be giving you paid holiday as a freelancer, but we all need a break. Assess when you are likely to be quietest, or simply when you would like to have some time off. Mark it on your calendar and let clients know well in advance that you will be on holiday during those dates. It's not just you who needs a break. Your family will also thank you for the vacation, especially if they have to share the house with a grumpy, overworked freelancer.

Becoming a reliable supplier

It's a dog-eat-dog world for freelancers. There is growing competition for work and you're only as good as your last job. You'll hear those clichés a lot as a freelancer, because they are largely true.

Reliability is the asset most prized by clients among their freelancers, and it's the key to a successful freelance career. Sporadic brilliance gets trumped by everyday, nose-to-the-grindstone dependability every time. You are called on as an intermittent resource, so you have to be on the money every time.

So what makes you Mr or Ms Reliable?

Deliver good work

It almost goes without saying that the standard of your work should be universally high. However, it's easy to let it dip at times. The reasons this might happen could include taking on too much work, failure to understand or abide by your brief, or a lack of experience in a particular area.

Protect your personal brand by ensuring that you don't fall down in these areas. There can be a temptation to BANJO some jobs. This means 'bang a nasty job out' where you rush something you're not enjoying to get it off your plate. Try to resist this, as it could simply lead to you being taken off a company's freelance roster. Plus, you will probably still have to put right the substandard work that you were commissioned for.

Always deliver to the brief you are given

If the brief is unclear, question it and clarify any areas that you don't understand. Make sure that you send your questions by email and get a reply in writing. This will ensure that everybody is aware of what has been commissioned and that there are no misunderstandings at a later date. You will do everyone a favour in the long run.

This doesn't mean that you can't question a brief as you go along. As you do a job, it may become clear that a brief needs to be amended. Be proactive in contacting the client if you think this needs to happen.

Stay in contact and keep the client abreast of developments

It can be easy to go into head-down mode and crack on with a project without letting the client know what is going on. With longer projects especially, it pays to have some sort of regular reporting built in to your relationship. This can be as simple as a weekly phone call or email to update them.

Even if there is nothing to tell them, by keeping them informed you give them confidence that they can go on with their job, safe in the knowledge that you are on top of yours. The project you have may be just one part of a bigger project that the client is orchestrating, so if there are problems at your end, they may have to make adjustments elsewhere along the chain. Don't leave them in the dark and don't leave it to the last minute to break bad news.

When things do go awry, don't bring problems without solutions

Things do go wrong sometimes and clients should accept that, but as the person closest to a particular part of the project you may be in the best position to suggest what to do next. Even if your suggestion isn't taken up, you have demonstrated that you are not the sort of person who sits idly by and waits for somebody else to sort things out.

Be a self-starter who doesn't need too much hand-holding

The nature of freelancing is that you are entrusted with a task because a client doesn't have the manpower or resources in-house to do it themselves. As such, they expect you to get on with the job without needing to ask them questions every five minutes. Remember, they have jobs of their own to do. The briefing stage is the time at which you should iron out any queries you have. This doesn't mean you can never ask any questions, but try to avoid the dumb and obvious ones.

Somebody who can turn work round quickly is prized by clients

There are times when clients need something done speedily, and they will tend to go to people who have been able to this in the past. Working to a tight deadline will enable you to get into the client's good books, and you should be able to charge a premium into the bargain. Just don't sacrifice speed for quality.

Be flexible and fit in

Freelancers are usually solitary workers, but an ability to slot seamlessly into a team is a definite asset, particularly for those freelancers who work shifts. Moving from workplace to workplace is difficult as they all have slightly different quirks and working practices. If you can hit the ground running and not rub up the permanent staff the wrong way in the process, then you'll be called back in future. Don't shrink into the background and let things happen around you. Ask what you can do to help, make suggestions about what you can do next if you come to the end of one task, and let people know that you are available. You don't have to make everybody tea to fit in. Doing your job effectively and efficiently is enough.

Provide value for money

Note that this isn't always about being the cheapest freelancer in town. Value is about providing a good service for a fair level of remuneration, so if you can make the case that your skills, experience and talent are worth a higher rate than other freelancers, then you still provide value for money.

Try to continually add value to what you offer

You can do this by moving out of your comfort zone and adding to your set of skills. No business stands still, so it makes sense to stay abreast of developments in your industry and 'skill up' accordingly. It takes time to add skills, so try and set aside a little time each week or every month for career development. Adding new skills will also open up a wider choice of jobs, which could pay better and potentially lead you into new and interesting areas. Speak to clients and other freelancers about the kind of skills they think are important for the future of work in your sector. There is no point learning something that is rapidly becoming redundant.

Monitor client satisfaction levels and act on feedback

You can do this by having a quick chat with somebody at the end of a project, or you may wish to take a more formal poll of client feeling. You could include a link to an online survey, such as Survey Monkey (www.surveymonkey.com) with your invoice. By ensuring that a job has been completed to the satisfaction of a client, you are also putting yourself in a good position to pick up your next job from the company.

Continue the after-sales service

Use effective administration processes, such as providing an ongoing paper trail for the client. Invoices and reports should be produced professionally and promptly.

Keep a dialogue going with clients to keep them informed about what you are doing

An email with recent project announcements, for example, will ensure that your clients know about any developments in your business and will also keep you on their radar at times when they are not working with you.

Top tips for freelancers

Freelance production editor David Powning on the rules that freelancers must obey to be Mr or Ms Reliable.

- **Go the extra mile.** Don't start crying if you're asked to stay a bit late or work during the lunch hour, especially on press day. It counts for a lot, especially in these times of cutbacks and skeleton staff, and the next time the publication needs a freelancer I guarantee you'll be near the front of the queue, a long way ahead of the clock watchers. Yes, you have rights, but don't get all French about it and start waving your *Book of Working Conditions* in people's faces. They're under pressure, they don't want to hear it – they just want your help. You enjoy the work; get on with it.
- **You're a lone wolf.** Accept that some people don't like you. The phrase 'f***ing freelancers' is common currency because we're not part of the gang, and we perhaps don't have the brand loyalty that full-timers cling to until a better job comes up. So when someone lays into freelancers in your presence, and it's as if you're not actually in the room, just keep your head down and imagine them on the toilet.
- **Keeping that head down.** When you're working somewhere for the first time, don't go in guns a-blazing, trying to dazzle them with the force of your exciting personality. Take the time to see how the land lies, and work out the 'dynamics' of the office before you start to contribute. This usually helps prevent you from making verbal gaffes that some sensitive doily will find offensive, and will enable you to fit seamlessly into the team. Working environments all have their own gentle rhythms; don't barge in banging your own drum. If you do they will start emailing each other behind your back, and you will never see them again.
- **Don't ever be late.** Unless it's one of your regular gigs and genuine tragedy has befallen you. It's a curious thing, but when full-timers are a bit late getting to the office and trawl out their excuses about

the transport system, despite the fact that they reek of booze and are partially blind, everyone shrugs or makes light of it. If as a freelancer, however, you make the same mistake, you are a feckless waster who clearly doesn't appreciate the gilded opportunities that life is affording you. You won't be able to laugh it off, so unless you're bleeding heavily and/or missing a limb, get there on time. And even if you are bleeding, still make the effort.

- **Turn work down.** You heard me. Value yourself. If you get a call saying 'You've been recommended, but we don't have a very big budget, so the daily rate is below the norm,' politely explain that you're good at your job (hence the recommendation) and will a) go the extra mile b) keep your head down and c) turn up on time, even if bleeding. Working for cut-rates is pointless – it doesn't help you or freelancers in general, and you might as well go and do something else if people think they can get you on the cheap. Let them work their way through all those freelancers who will work for peanuts, and see what kind of standard they get. Then later you'll receive another phone call and, hey presto, the daily rate just went back up to where it should have been in the first place.
- **Finally, take pride in what you do** – above everything.

Getting repeat work

The things that make you a reliable freelancer will help you to get repeat work. You want to avoid having to pitch for every single job individually. There simply aren't enough hours in the day for this and you will quickly burn out.

As a freelancer, you will probably find that the 80:20 rule applies. In other words, 80% of your business comes from 20% of your clients. You need to focus your efforts on ensuring that the all-important 20% of your client base is happy with your work, and look for areas where you can expand what you offer them.

Long-term relationships are important in business, and especially so in freelancing where personal contacts are so much more important. Clients are not dealing with an anonymous sales department, they are dealing with you directly.

It is a universal truth in business that it's more cost-effective to keep hold of a customer or client than it is to gain a new one. Look at your accounts and add up the value of your top two or three clients. Now try to imagine how you would fill the gap if you lost one or two of them. It's scary, isn't it?

You can work with a good client for years which will provide you with ongoing work. They may also continue to use your services when they move to new workplaces, so make sure that you stay in touch with them. There's nothing worse than calling up a client organisation to find out that your main point of contact has moved on, and the old organisation won't tell you where. You then have to start from scratch in building a relationship with the company and proving your value to them.

You must gear your approach towards being honest and open with your clients. Always look to conclude any job by finding out if it has been achieved to the satisfaction of the client. If there have been issues, look to address them as quickly as possible.

Clients are also an excellent source of information about what their industry expects. Your market may be changing and you have to be able to continue to provide a compelling service. Tap into this resource.

Calendar of work

Find out about your clients' plans and attempt to provide a service that meets those plans. Many businesses work to a predictable calendar, when they are busy at a certain time of year and are committed to certain activities. Look at your past dealings with them to see if you can predict when there is a business opportunity for you, then get in early and pitch to them. For example, you might say: 'Last year I supplied you with this service. It's getting near that time again, so I was wondering if I could help you out with it this year.'

It is even better if you can confirm a future booking for work at the conclusion of a successful job. Why not suggest that you put something in the diary to ensure that you are available for their project in the future? Nearer the time you can confirm the booking and start to get into more detail about what is required this year.

As somebody coming to a project with past experience of what went on, you can suggest ways in which things could be slicker this year. There is always room for improvement, and by being proactive and constructive, you are adding value to your relationship with the client.

If the job has been concluded well, then use this as an opportunity to get more work. Sometimes simply asking if there is anything else you can do for the company can lead to another job. The client may have something that they are looking to outsource and your prompting, combined with their contentment with your recent work, may provide them with a custom-made solution.

Keep in touch

Make sure that you keep in contact with customers in some way. A round robin email may do the trick, or for more valuable clients you might want to take a more personal approach, such as meeting up for a coffee or a drink if you are near their offices. Give them some notice and use the meeting as a chance to update them on what you've been doing and any new skills you have acquired, as well as finding out what they have been up to. Sharing industry gossip can be a good way of demonstrating how plugged into their sector you are.

A big part of keeping work coming in is attending to personal relationships. There is a phrase 'people buy people', which you often hear in relation to service businesses. In other words, it means that we like to work with people who we like and who provide us with a good service.

Don't underestimate the importance of that personal link. It doesn't have to mean being obsequious or toadying, but can simply be about being polite and professional. Showing an interest in somebody as a person away from the workplace can also be a way of deepening a personal relationship. Do you have shared interests that you can talk about, for example? Dropping somebody a birthday or Christmas card, or enquiring how their kids are doing, are simple ways of helping to forge a link on a personal level.

Keep it cordial

We spend a huge amount of our lives working, and as freelancers it can sometimes be lonely. There is nothing wrong with making friends with a client, and it certainly won't harm your chances of continuing to work for them. However, remember where the line lies between friendship and business, and never expect to be given work simply because of a friendship.

This sort of approach cannot be forced. There are times when you will work for people that you don't like very much. At such times, you should act in a professional manner and deliver what the client requires. Don't let your personality get in the way of the business relationship. Keep your feelings to yourself, your head down and deliver the job to the best of your ability.

Don't burn your bridges with companies. After a particularly tough job you may be tempted to tell a business or its people that you never want to work with them again. It's better to take a deep breath, count to 10 and submit your invoice. Companies and personnel change, so don't storm out: a year down the line, the organisation could be completely different.

Formalising the relationship

If you find that you are getting a regular supply of work from one client, look to see if there is some way that you can formalise the relationship. For example, you could suggest that rather than having an ad hoc relationship you dedicate a set amount of time per week or month to a particular client.

Present this as a reasoned business case, emphasising how this approach will help both of you to make better use of your scarce time and resources. It may even save the client some money if they know that you are on their clock.

Teaming up with other freelancers

Networks have always been important, and are becoming increasingly so with the growing importance of social media and online linkages.

Partnering with other professionals in your field is a way to gain access to jobs that might be too big for you to handle on your own. A virtual team can come together to undertake bigger projects or more complex tasks where you lack certain skills.

Make contact with groups of freelancers and find out if this is something that they do. Look out for freelance Meetup or Jelly groups in your area. Find out about their areas of expertise and let them know about the areas you work in.

Being in touch with a network is also a good way of getting referral work. Groups may receive requests from clients looking for particular skills, and are in a position to pass on leads to you. Similarly, as part of the group, you can pass on information about jobs that you are not in a position to take up yourself.

The important thing to remember about freelancing is that you always need to be on the lookout for the next job. Loyalty can be non-existent for freelancers, and usually there is nothing to stop clients from cutting you loose at the end of a job. Never get complacent just because you are busy at the moment, and never stop pitching.

When freelancing turns into a business

The motivation to become a freelancer is very similar to that which motivates entrepreneurs. They are tired of working for somebody else. Perhaps they have spotted a gap in the market, and they think that they can make a better try of things going it alone rather than being stuck as a wage slave for somebody else.

If your freelance career really takes off, you may reach a crossroads where you have to decide whether or not to take the plunge and scale up the business beyond that of a one-man band.

How do you know if you are ready to expand?

The signs are pretty obvious. If you are regularly turning away valuable work because you are simply too busy, then the chances are that you could grow the business. However, before you commit to becoming a slightly bigger (though still small) business, you need to ask yourself a few questions.

Do you want to grow?

The reason you went freelance in the first place may have been to have a more straightforward existence. You may also have wanted less stress and a better work–life balance. Becoming the boss of a growing business will lead to a whole heap of new challenges you will have to face, not least hiring and managing staff. The first few years will be tough and there is a high chance that your enterprise could fail. It's a big change – do you really want to do it?

Can you do it?

The skills that have made you a great freelancer are not necessarily the same as those which will help you to build a profitable growing business. What skills will you need, and if you don't have them or can't obtain them, where will they come from?

Will it be profitable to grow?

With any growth plan, your costs will increase as you scale up the business with new staff, premises, equipment and marketing costs. Are the margins in your business enough to make your efforts worthwhile? At the end of the day, might it not be as profitable to stay as a one-man band?

What's the plan?

Business conditions are pretty good for you at the minute, which is why you are considering growing the business, but in the longer term you need a business plan that takes other eventualities into consideration. What are your targets for your first few years? How will the business develop in that time? What happens if business dips?

Can you grow and remain a one-man band?

You need more resources, but that doesn't mean that you have to become a bigger business in personnel terms. It may be possible to outsource more of your business to other people. Co-working or partnering may also allow you to take on bigger and more profitable jobs without relinquishing your freelance status. Is there another way ahead?

Writing a business plan

If you have asked yourself all of these questions and still think that you need to grow, then the first thing you need to do is look at your business plan. As a freelancer you may not have one, but as a small and growing enterprise, a business plan is an essential tool to develop your business.

A business plan is a written statement of your business; what you want to achieve, and how you plan to go about it. It should outline the structure of your business, the product or service, the customer, the growth potential and the financials.

As well as giving information about your business, your business plan should also inspire you for the future. It's a blueprint for what you want to achieve, and should give you a clear understanding of how you intend to get there. That's not to say it should act as a rigid prediction of every future occurrence. You can't control the future, and outside circumstances will have an effect. But a good plan should at least give you a clear direction to aim for.

Every business should have a plan. It helps you to define strategy and, if properly used, will help you involve and motivate key members of staff. It allows you to work out how to make your business a success and can help you avoid failure. It should outline a realistic target for how this can happen while remaining flexible enough to make changes along the way. By setting out a plan and some targets, you can also monitor your progress and get the business back on track fairly quickly if anything goes wrong.

If you need to borrow money, the business plan explains to your backers or bank how you will spend it and what the next stage is for your business. Regardless of whether you need outside funding or not, it's always a good idea to set out your ideas on paper, even if it's just a case of looking at your idea from the point of view of a potential investor. It can really highlight areas you haven't yet considered and help you form a realistic estimate of how much it's all going to cost, and in what kind of time frame you can expect to become fully open for business.

Business structures

As a freelancer you are probably a sole trader – a business that is owned and controlled by one person – but as a business you may want to opt for a different legal structure.

Partnership

This is when two or more people combine to form a business unit. There was previously a restriction stating that a maximum of 20 partners was allowed, but this has now been lifted. Each partner receives a percentage of the return of the business, depending upon how much they invested.

As with sole traders, partners are also responsible for all the debts incurred by the business no matter which partner incurs those debts. Creditors can take your personal assets to pay off debts incurred by other partners if necessary.

Before embarking on a partnership, you should ensure that there is a partnership agreement in place. This is a legal agreement covering such issues as the structure of the business, roles of individuals, and exit routes for those wishing to leave the partnership.

Limited company

A limited or limited liability company is very different from a sole trader. If you're a sole trader or partner, you can be held personally liable – outstanding debts can be met from your personal assets.

Registering and running a limited company requires more legal administration than a sole trader business or partnership. However, while the business owner is personally responsible for any debts incurred by a sole trader business, a limited company is a separate legal entity to the company directors. Profits and losses belong to the company, and the business can continue regardless of the death, resignation or bankruptcy of the shareholders or people who run the business.

Limited companies pay corporation tax on their profits, and company directors are taxed as employees in the same way as any other people you employ to work for the company.

Your personal financial risk is restricted to how much you invested in the company and any guarantees you gave when raising finance for the business. However, if the company fails and you have not carried out your duties as a company director, you could be liable for debts as well as being disqualified from acting as a director in another company.

How to register a limited company

1. Decide whether you can register the business yourself or if you need outside help. Unless you've done it before, you may need to engage the services of a solicitor, accountant, chartered secretary or a company formation agent. These can be found online, with Companies House including a list of agents (www. companieshouse.gov.uk/toolsToHelp/formationAgents.shtml).

2. Decide on the company officers. A private company must have appointed company officers at all times. Company officers are the formally named directors and company secretary as stated in the articles of association. It is a legal requirement for company officers to be in place at all times, and for their names and current addresses to be written on the registration documents. If there is a change in company officers, Companies House must be informed straight away. According to The Companies Act 2006, all private limited companies must have at least one director. A private company does not need to have a secretary unless the company's articles of association require it. Articles of association are the internal rules for running the company and can include such information as when annual general meetings are held, how directors are appointed, and how shares are issued. The Companies House website includes downloadable templates of articles: www.companieshouse.gov.uk/about/modelArticles/modelArticles.shtml.

3. Choose a name for the company. The name you choose for your company must feature the word 'limited' or 'ltd' at the end. It must not be made up of certain sensitive words or expressions without the consent of the Secretary of State or relevant government department. Neither should it imply a connection with central or local government, or be offensive. It cannot be the same or similar to another company name. You can search the index of names at Companies House.

4. File the correct documents with Companies House. You need to send the following documents to Companies House:

- Form IN01 containing the name, registered address, secretary (if applicable) and directors, subscriber details, and share capital information.

- Memorandum of association

- Articles of association.

Hiring somebody else

If your workload has become too onerous and you've decided you want to grow your business, it's time to consider hiring your first employee.

The signs you need to do so include the following.

→ Stress: you're constantly left feeling that you can't finish the work on time.

→ You're exhausted: a few late nights on deadline are fine, but you can't continually burn the candle at both ends.

→ Your family is not seeing you: ask them if they think you are working too hard.

→ There's no downtime: everyone deserves a beer and a catch-up with their mates occasionally. When was the last time you managed it?

→ You feel demoralised.

→ Your work's quality is declining and you are missing deadlines.

→ You are losing clients as a result of this.

If you decide that you do want to hire your first member of staff, you should be aware that you are letting yourself in for a whole lot of red tape. This isn't a reason not to hire somebody, but it could mean that you are better off seeking advice from an HR or business consultant before you become an employer.

You need to be aware of the law on:

-↗ employee rights

-↗ equal opportunities

-↗ health and safety

-↗ maternity rights

-↗ minimum pay

-↗ PAYE and National Insurance

-↗ sick leave

-↗ working hours.

To take somebody on as your employee, you will need to register with HMRC as an employer. This should be done at least four weeks before pay day and can be done online, by email or by phone.

> **Startups Tip**
> The Businesslink website (businesslink.gov.uk) includes an interactive tool that takes you through the process of adding an employee.

Finding the right person

Finding the right person for your fledgling business is an important task. As a small business, personal chemistry is as important as hiring somebody who can do the job. Define the roles you are recruiting for as precisely as you can, and bear in mind that a job description must work both ways. It's not only an opportunity to attract candidates – it must also enable applicants to decide whether they are right for your business. Attracting unsuitable candidates wastes your time and money.

When you have decided what your needs are, you have to try to attract the right person. When you advertise, include, for example, the position that's on offer, and whether the role is permanent/contract and full time/part time. What responsibilities will you expect the recruit to carry out and what level of experience must be met? As part of the business recruitment process, outline the benefits of joining your company. It's a good idea to include the personal attributes you are seeking as this can help you narrow your recruitment choice.

The cheapest way to handle staff recruitment is through the grapevine – let the people you work with, your suppliers and other business contacts know you are looking to recruit. Turn to your local job centre for recruitment advice – services are free and they can also arrange space for you to carry out interviews if necessary.

Press ads are an expensive choice when it comes to recruitment, so plan them carefully – ensure the ad stands out and that it does not fall foul of discriminatory rules relating to gender, race or disability. You must not refer to age, race or physical abilities or use language that might suggest you are seeking somebody young or old, as you could be accused of discriminatory practice.

Staff recruitment agencies often have steep placement fees, but these can be negotiated – particularly if you decide to use them on a regular basis. If the recruitment is for a very senior role, consider hiring a headhunter who knows your sector well on a project basis.

 ## Checklist

- ☑ Consider your prices carefully: you don't want to undervalue your work, nor do you want to put clients off.

- ☑ Work on your time management skills: completing jobs well and on time is key to a successful freelance career.

- ☑ Become known as a reliable supplier: deliver what you promised, when you promised it.

Checklist

☑ Keep in touch with clients to build up your calendar of repeat work.

☑ Once you're established and getting steady work, you might want to consider turning your solo career into a business.

↻ CHAPTER 7

Admin

📖 What's in this chapter?

Doing paid work is only part of the job of a freelancer. In order to keep the wheels turning, you must learn to attend to a host of other essential administrative tasks. It may not sound the most exciting part of freelancing, but without it your career will not thrive. In this chapter we will cover:

→ registering for VAT
→ National Insurance contributions
→ maintaining records
→ tax breaks for freelancers
→ tax returns
→ expenses
→ invoicing
→ getting paid
→ holidays.

The paper trail

Unless you are a freelance bookkeeper, you probably didn't start working for yourself to do paperwork. However, attending to the paper trail is one of the most important parts of your job.

In employment, that's somebody else's job, but now that you are a one-man band, it's down to you to keep track of things. Without accurate bookkeeping you won't know if you're making a profit or not. Your sales, profits, invoices, and other crucial bits of paperwork are your business intelligence. They are an indicator of how your business is going, where there is an opportunity to make more money, and who your key clients are.

This is seriously useful information, don't neglect it.

Be organised

When it comes to admin, the important thing is to be organised. Try to set up procedures for the working week to help you manage your time and workload. Beyond the week, keep a diary of important dates, such as deadlines for filing tax returns.

Don't think of admin as just an encumbrance to the business of making money. Think of it as an important part of your job. A disorganised set-up will slow you down and make you less efficient. You should have clients' contact details to hand in an index or database which can contain pertinent notes from previous jobs. Setting up a system of computerised alerts will mean you need never miss an appointment.

Depending on your line of work, you may need various documents such as contracts, terms and conditions, invoices and briefing sheets. Make sure that you have these in place when you start your freelance career – they will make things a lot simpler later on. You can find template documents at various websites, or freelance friends may allow you to adapt theirs. See Appendix 3 for a sample brief and Appendix 4 for an example of terms and conditions.

Work out how your paperwork fits into your workflow. For some businesses, this will be relatively simple. For example, a freelance journalist will receive a brief, agree to it, complete the commission and invoice the client. There isn't too much paperwork involved in that.

For other freelancers, the admin burden may be more onerous, with client reports, sign offs, and confidentiality agreements to deal with and keep on file.

Whatever the case, the important thing to remember is to stay on top of things. Allocating an hour or so every week, or even fortnight, to admin is a lot easier than being panicked into doing a year's worth of filing over a weekend. Make admin part of your routine.

Doing your own accounts

As we have already mentioned in Chapter 3, it can be a daunting prospect to give up a full-time job and find yourself responsible for your own accounts. As an employee your tax and National Insurance are deducted at source via PAYE. Now there is no buffer between you and the almighty HM Revenue & Customs. It's tempting to say that there's no need to worry and that the entire bookkeeping process is child's play, but that wouldn't be strictly true. If it were, accountants wouldn't be paid so well. But the HMRC is not – unless provoked – a bullying, authoritarian organisation.

On the contrary, HMRC aims to help businesses manage their accounts as effectively as possible. To this end, the organisation publishes regular newsletters and leaflets giving tips and guidance on bookkeeping, and has teams of advisors on hand to help out over the phone should you run into difficulties.

Before you launch your own business, it can be worth talking to the local offices of HMRC (find your nearest one here: www.hmrc.gov. uk/enq). Call them, make an appointment, explain the details of your business plan and ask them exactly what you need to do. They'll provide you with advice, relevant leaflets and a selection of forms – such as VAT registration – that you should complete before beginning trading.

This is important. If you start off with all the necessary information, it will make the bookkeeping process much easier. It also helps to have a contact within the local offices who you can call whenever you run into any difficulties.

If you're setting up as a sole trader then your bookkeeping work can be kept to a minimum. There's the added advantage that sole traders pay less tax than any other class of working people, although you have to be careful that you don't fall foul of the IR35 regulation (see p. 67).

As we mentioned in Chapter 3, when you start out freelancing, you need to register as self-employed and are then responsible for your self-assessment tax returns and VAT payments.

HMRC works on the basis that 'if it looks like an employee, it's an employee'. This was introduced to prevent contractors working on site for single clients for long periods of time, effectively acting as employees but invoicing as sole traders or single-employee limited companies. The ruling has been challenged a number of times, and remains contentious, but for now it remains and must be considered.

You could manage your accounts by hand, but it's easier to do it using a computer. A spreadsheet will suffice, containing columns for income, expenditure and VAT (if you are VAT-registered).

Registering for VAT

If your turnover is expected to be more than £77,000 a year, then VAT will need to be applied to your earnings. To register for VAT you'll need to download and complete form VAT1 available from HMRC (www.hmrc.gov.uk/vat/index.htm).

The VAT forms are very simple – just a single page, in fact – and usually work in your favour. This is because although you must pay VAT on any income generated, you can claim back VAT paid on some goods and services, such as office supplies, vehicle servicing, fuel and so on (see p. 210 for more on expenses). So the extra accounting is definitely worth it and even companies whose turnover is less than the VAT limit can still register voluntarily.

> ### Startups Tip
> Not all products and services attract the standard 20% VAT rate, so it's worth contacting your local HMRC office to request one of their introductory guides, which will explain the basics of VAT accounting. If that's not enough, you can also enrol on a brief course, again run by HMRC, which will go into greater detail.

Try to keep track of changes to tax regulations. This means listening to the entire Budget speech, not just the part about cigarettes, alcohol and petrol. An accountant should do this for you, but it doesn't hurt to know about VAT limits, changes in basic tax rates and changes to the company car regulations yourself.

Additional VAT forms you may need to download

If you're registering a partnership you'll also be required to fill in VAT 2, although this is not as yet available to complete online. A partnership is a legal entity where you share the risks and rewards equally with somebody else. A freelancer might do this in order to take on bigger or more complex jobs. However, it will also mean more complex legal and tax affairs so it's not a common undertaking.

If you're planning on doing business internationally, you can download the form to register for VAT for acquisitions (VAT 1B), although this cannot be completed online, and so must be sent by post to HMRC.

National Insurance contributions

As a sole trader, you'll also have to talk to HMRC about National Insurance contributions; the easiest way to handle these is by setting up a Direct Debit. The amounts involved are quite small. Self-employed workers have to pay Class 2 National Insurance payments. For the financial year 2012/13, Class 2 National Insurance contributions are paid at a flat rate of £2.65 a week. However, if your profits are expected to be less than £5,595 you may not have to pay any Class 2 National Insurance contributions. Self-employed workers also have to pay Class 4 National

Insurance contributions. These are paid as a percentage of your annual taxable profits, which is 9% on profits between £7,605 and £42,475, and a further 2% on profits over that amount. You will pay Class 4 National Insurance contributions when you pay your income tax. However, this can be settled with your tax return at the end of the year.

Startups Tip

More information can be found at:

■ www.hmrc.gov.uk/payinghmrc/class2nics.htm

■ www.hmrc.gov.uk/working/intro/class4.htm

Self-assessment tax return

Once you're registered with HMRC, they'll send you a letter telling you to file your tax return every year in April. This relates to the previous tax year, from 6 April to the following 5 April.

If you are self-employed, you have to fill in a self-assessment tax return every year. HMRC will send you the paper forms you'll need, or you can complete your tax return online. Usually, HMRC will send your self-assessment tax return to you in April. However, if yours doesn't arrive by the end of April, contact your tax office.

You'll be asked for details about profits from your business and other income that you'll have to pay tax on – such as rental income. This is used to work out how much in tax and National Insurance contributions you have to pay. You must provide the correct information and get it to HMRC on time.

If this is the first tax return you've completed, you'll need to fill in a self-assessment registration form first. Make sure you have your National Insurance number to hand when doing this. This involves completing a CWF1 form to inform HMRC about your business, which will also register you for self-assessment.

Once this is done, HMRC will set up tax records for you and will send you a Unique Taxpayer Reference (UTR).

Self-assessment payment deadlines

If you owe any money by the end of the tax year (April), you must pay that amount by 31 January the following year. The payment deadline is the same whether you file online or on paper. You will need to pay one or both of the following:

-➔ the balancing payment (the balance of tax you owe for the previous year)

-➔ the first of two 'payments on account' (advance payments for the current tax year).

You should receive a self-assessment statement that shows the amount due; however, if you don't receive this before payment is due, you'll need to work out the tax due yourself by registering for self-assessment online and using the 'view account' option. If you're asked to make payments on account, your deadline for making your second payment is 31 July.

Self-assessment forms

If you usually receive a paper tax return, HMRC will always send you the core pages of the tax return – forms SA100 and SA101. You may also have to fill in some supplementary pages, depending on your circumstances. If you're self-employed you'll need to complete either page SA103S (if your turnover was below £70,000) or SA103F (if your turnover was £70,000 or more).

If you're self-employed in a business partnership, you'll need to complete either page SA104S (for partnerships that only have trading income along with taxed bank and building society interest or alternative finance receipts) or page SA104F (for all other types of partnership income). These forms detail your share of the partnership's profit or loss.

You may need page SA102 if you also work as an employee.

Filing your tax return online

Paying VAT and taxes are now a part of most small businesses. In the past completing a tax return would be a long-winded paper exercise.

Now government departments are encouraging all of us to make payments and submissions using the internet, and since 1 April 2011, all companies and organisations have to file their company tax return online for any accounting period ending after 31 March 2010. From the same date, companies and organisations will also have to pay any corporation tax and related payments due electronically (for example by Direct Debit).

What are online submissions?

Online submissions are simply the completion of forms using the internet, instead of completing them manually and posting them off. By encouraging online submission, government departments can reduce the paper workload on their staff and hopefully reduce costs. Data that you complete online in a form gets put into a central database and then processed, rather than being hand copied or scanned into systems.

For example, the following can be submitted to HM Revenue & Customs online:

→ corporation tax

→ PAYE forms and returns

→ self-assessment forms.

Local authorities may also enable you to pay bills such as business rates online. Other government bodies that issue grants will often expect an online application. This follows the basic model as used to pay taxes or VAT. Check with the grant provider to see what support they can give you for online submissions.

Why should I bother with online submissions?

Online filing is secure and accurate, and the software automatically calculates your tax. You also get an immediate acknowledgment when HMRC receives your tax return and faster repayment. By submitting documents online, a business can save money and operate more efficiently. Once you have the computers and connections in place there is no additional cost to online submissions compared to paper submissions.

Records

As well as the responsibility to register as self-employed with HMRC, you are now required to keep adequate records of your work, so that you can fill in your tax return fully and accurately. Filling out your tax return means keeping track of all invoices (along with the dates they were issued and the dates they were paid) and all receipts for work-related transactions, including any ground rent, telephone bills, heating and electricity bills and so on. If you work from home, some of your household expenditure may be tax-deductible.

Keeping track of income and expenses

As a sole trader you have to keep track of monthly income and expenditure, which means holding on to all invoices and receipts. The more detailed records you keep, the easier it will be to answer any questions that HMRC may have. You'll need all of these records to fill in the tax return form each year.

Keep the paperwork

No matter where you store it, keep a record of everything. Keep bank statements, credit card slips and bills, invoices and payment receipts. You can use a shoe box or something similar and dump all of your paperwork in there. Get into the habit of asking for receipts for everything you spend. It may not all be tax deductible, but if you have the receipt then you will be able to claim against it. Remember to empty out your wallet, purse or bag regularly. You'll be surprised what work-related purchases you have made and then forgotten about. Have a separate envelope for expenses each month to make things a bit more straightforward.

Keep a check

At least twice a year, if not quarterly, have a spring clean of your records. Check payments and credits against your bank or credit card statements. Make sure the right money is moving in and out of your account. We have all heard the stories of people losing thousands of pounds in bank 'errors'.

Keep the books

If possible, enter everything into a book and tally everything by numbering invoices, payment receipts and payments in. This tedious paperwork costs heavily in hours spent by the accountant. If you do not have the time or inclination to do this, then try and find a bookkeeper whose hourly rates will be lower than those of an accountant.

Saving for the taxman

In a perfect world, every self-employed person would put aside at least one quarter of every cheque they receive, ready for the tax bill. In reality it does not happen like that, but bear in mind that the tax bill will arrive and you will need to have set aside sufficient money. It can be a long time between registering as self-employed and having to pay your first tax bill, and you can end up sticking your head in the sand and thinking it will never come. But when it does, you need to have the funds to hand or a very good excuse, or you will face stringent penalty payments.

It helps to set aside a certain amount of each payment for tax from the moment you invoice it or at the moment your receive payment. That way you will not mentally spend the money on anything else. But it is safer still to save regularly – perhaps have a special 'tax' account which you put a direct debit into monthly. This can be an interest bearing account, so at the end of the year you might even get a drink out of it.

Startups Tip

HMRC has produced a guide to record keeping, which is a good starting point to understanding what records you need to keep, how you should keep them, and what the penalties are if you do not keep adequate records.

Find them here:

- www.hmrc.gov.uk/sa/rk-bk1.pdf
- www.hmrc.gov.uk/factsheet/record-keeping.pdf.

What business records do I need to keep?

Your basic business records must include:

➔ a record of all your sales and takings

➔ a record of all your purchases and expenses.

You or your accountant can use these records to create a profit and loss account – which shows the sales income you've received and the expenses you've paid, and what profit/loss you've actually made. The more detailed records you keep, the easier it will be to answer any questions that HMRC has about your tax return.

Business records you need to keep are:

➔ annual accounts, including profit and loss accounts (the balance between revenue coming in from work and business expenses you accrue).

➔ bank statements and paying-in slips

➔ cash books and other account books

➔ orders and delivery notes

➔ purchase and sales books

➔ records of daily takings such as till rolls

➔ relevant business correspondence.

VAT records you need to keep are:

➔ records of all the goods and services you buy or sell

➔ copies of all sales invoices you issue

➔ all purchase invoices for items you buy

➔ all credit notes and debit notes you receive

➔ copies of all credit notes and debit notes you issue

→ any self-billing agreements (an arrangement where a customer raises the sales invoice and sends it to you with payment) you make as a supplier

→ copies of self-billing agreements you make as a customer and name, address and VAT registration number of the supplier

→ records of any goods you give away or take from stock for your private use including rate and amount of VAT

→ records of any goods or services bought for which you cannot reclaim the VAT

→ any documents dealing with special VAT treatment

→ records of any goods you export

→ records of any taxable self-supplies you make – for example, if you sell cars and you use one of your cars in stock for business purposes

→ any adjustments such as corrections to your accounts or amended VAT invoices

→ a VAT account.

How long must I keep my paperwork?

You must normally keep your business records for 5 years after the normal filing deadline of 31 January. This date applies even if you've sent in a paper tax return. For example, for a 2011/12 tax return filed on or before 31 January 2013, you must keep your records until 31 January 2018.

> **Startups Tip**
> As long as your VAT records meet the requirements laid down by HMRC, you may keep them in whatever format you prefer (paper and/ or electronic).

But if HMRC sent you – or you sent back – your tax return very late, you may need to keep your records for longer. You need to keep them until the later date of:

-> five years after the normal filing deadline

-> 15 months after the date you sent your tax return.

You may also need to keep your records for longer if a check into your tax return has been started – in this case, you'll need to keep your records until HMRC writes and tells you they've finished the check.

HMRC calendar

Efficient record keeping and the cumbersome tax return is the bane of thousands of self-employed people's lives. However, if you know exactly what you need to submit and when you need to do it, things get a lot easier.

Make note of the following dates: write them in your calendar or set up reminders on your computer. Whatever you do, don't ignore them. If you can plan ahead you'll find the whole process far less daunting.

6 April 2012: First day of the new tax year
This is where everything starts from new. You'll need to start organising detailed records from this date to be able to do your tax return for the financial year 2012/13.

31 July 2012: Deadline for second self-assessment payment on account for 2011/12 tax year
If it's your first year of trading this won't apply to you, but if you've already done one tax return you'll be given an estimated amount to pay HMRC based on what you earned the previous tax year. This payment goes towards your total tax owed for the year 2011/12. You will already have made your first payment on account for that tax year back in January.

31 October 2012: Deadline for submitting PAPER self-assessment tax returns for 2011/12 tax year
If you want to submit your return on paper, you need to have it in by this date; otherwise, you could be fined. However, if you miss this date you still have until 31 January to file it online.

31 January 2013: Deadline for submitting ONLINE self-assessment tax return for 2011/12 tax year
This is the final date you can submit your tax return for the year 2011/12. Any returns submitted after this are subject to fines and interest on any late tax payments.

31 January 2013: Deadline for paying 2011/12 'Balancing Charge'

31 January 2013: Deadline for first self-assessment payment on account for 2012/13 tax year

HMRC penalties for late payment of tax

- One day late: a fixed penalty of £100. This applies even if you have no tax to pay or have paid the tax you owe.
- Three months late: £10 for each following day – up to a 90 day maximum of £900. This is as well as the fixed penalty above.
- Six months late: £300 or 5% of the tax due, whichever is the higher. This is as well as the penalties above.
- 12 months late: £300 or 5% of the tax due, whichever is the higher. In serious cases you may be asked to pay up to 100% of the tax due instead. These are in addition to the penalties above.

Startups Tip
Penalties can be pretty stiff – under-assessment of tax can result in a penalty of up to 30% of the difference between the estimated and the actual amount of tax, so make sure you get it right!

A visit from the taxman

If you're a freelancer working from home, it's a good idea to keep your house in order tax-wise: legislation relating to inspection means that you can expect a visit from the taxman at any time.

HM Revenue & Custom powers extend to allowing inspectors to enter any business premises – unannounced – to check the 'tax position' of any individual or company. Impromptu inspections can be carried out whether a tax return has been made or not, and can take place within a return period that has not yet closed.

Business people and sole traders who claim expenses for 'use of home as an office' should be aware that HMRC inspectors even have the right to enter their home to check on business records.

The legislative changes, which came into effect from 1 April 2009, are part of HMRC's continuing programme to better co-ordinate inspection work across corporation tax, VAT and PAYE. The new rules aim to modernise and align statute and practice across the whole range of taxes and duties.

Appeals against notices are much more difficult under the new regime. You cannot appeal a request for statutory records, for instance, as HMRC has an absolute right of access to statutory records.

The new powers also make it easier for HMRC to carry out systems audits, because taxpayers are obliged to provide reasonable assistance to HMRC when looking at computer records for the purpose of checking a tax position.

Much of the discretion formerly exercised by HMRC in not charging penalties has been removed by these legislative changes. HMRC can use its new powers to charge penalties in relation to any tax position which gets adjusted where the taxpayer cannot show that reasonable care was taken in making the return.

The new legislation provides statutory bandings for penalties too, and penalties could now be chargeable as a result of technical changes, such as the removal of group relief from the penalty calculation, the introduction of cash penalties for adjustments to losses, and timing differences.

Auditing

The percentage of companies audited each year by HMRC is quite small, but the organisation has effective ways of tracking suspicious returns. The auditing process is thorough and time-consuming, since all receipts and invoices must be checked against the returns and shown to the investigating accountant. Also, the Statute of Limitations is biased in the auditors' favour, so you may have to dig out paperwork going back many years.

Because of this, you may want to take out auditing insurance with your accountant. The work involved during an audit is considerable – allow for three days at the very least – and could become very expensive if you pay your accountant by the hour.

Ultimately, you should remember that you're expected to account for every single business-related penny spent; this includes invoices for trade magazines and newspapers, for example. Although there may be some discretionary leeway, you are expected to show each month's transactions in sufficient detail that your profit and loss, income and expenditure – and therefore tax – can be clearly calculated.

Tax breaks for freelancers

HMRC allows various deductions, reliefs and allowances that freelancers can use to reduce their tax bill. Whatever your job, you'll rack up costs as a result of running your business. When it comes to year end, your profits are your income less expenses, and you only get taxed on your profits, so the higher your expenses, the lower your tax bill.

These must be expenses that are valid for the running of your business. You may be asked to provide evidence that you actually incurred the expenses and the expense was wholly necessary for your business if asked by HM Revenue & Customs, so don't be tempted to fiddle the accounts to pay less tax.

You can deduct much of your business expenditure to work out your profits – but you can't deduct private expenditure. You can also claim special reliefs for certain 'capital expenditure' – a one-off expenditure to buy or improve an asset you keep and use for your business, such as a new computer, phone or camera.

You can usually get deductions, reliefs and allowances for the current tax year and for the previous 4 years, although some have a shorter time limit for claiming.

Types of expenditure

Expenditure will usually fall into three different types. Each type has different rules for tax relief.

Capital expenditure

Expenditure on buying, creating or improving a business asset that you keep to earn the profits of your business is capital expenditure. So, the cost of buying a van for your business is capital expenditure but the cost of hiring it isn't.

Other examples of capital expenditure include the cost of buying business premises, machinery, computers, fixtures and furniture.

You won't be able to get tax relief for all types of capital expenditure. And if you can, there are special rules for how you can claim it.

Business expenditure

You can get tax relief for your business expenditure as long as it's not:

-> capital expenditure

-> non-allowable, for example entertaining expenditure.

To be allowable expenditure, it must be exclusively for carrying on and earning the profits of your business. You can get some private benefit from the expenditure and still get tax relief for the amount spent for your business, as long as either:

-> the private benefit was incidental

-> you can identify and separate the expenditure between business and private purposes.

So, if you can separate car expenditure between business and private purposes, the business part is allowable. You can deduct the full amount of your allowable business expenditure from your business income to work out your taxable profits.

Private expenditure

This is what you spend on your day-to-day living expenses, including the amounts you take from your business as a wage, or 'drawings'. You can't get tax relief for private expenditure.

Allowable and non-allowable business expenses

A business expense is allowable if it is wholly and exclusively for business purposes. The most common expenses that are normally allowable include:

→ administration costs

→ cost of stock

→ finance costs

→ motor and travel expenses

→ payroll costs

→ premises costs

→ professional fees repairs.

Key expenses, allowances and reliefs

The expenses, allowances and reliefs that you can get vary from business to business. The key ones are listed below, but specifics will depend on what you do for a living.

Capital allowances

You can get capital allowances on the cost of:

→ fixtures and fittings: includes shelves, furniture, electrical and plumbing fittings

⇢ plant and machinery: includes cars, vans, computers, equipment, tools

⇢ some buildings: includes industrial and agricultural buildings.

If you are self-employed, you must claim any capital allowances you are entitled to and wish to claim in your self-assessment Income Tax return. The claim must normally be made within 12 months after the 31 January filing deadline for the return. First-year allowances, some of which are also known as enhanced capital allowances, are currently available to businesses on the expenditure on certain items, such as energy-saving and water-efficient equipment, cars with very low carbon dioxide emissions, and goods vehicles with zero carbon emissions. These allowances enable you to make a claim for up to 100% of the cost of the item against your business profits in the year of purchase.

WANT TO KNOW MORE...

More information on allowances is available on the Business Link website: http://bit.ly/eswYBv.

Motoring expenses

You can deduct the cost of using your car for business purposes. There are two ways of working out how much you can deduct:

⇢ a fixed rate for each mile travelled on business, using fixed mileage rates (currently 45p a mile up to the first 10,000 miles and 25p per mile after that)

⇢ the actual expenses, worked out using detailed records of business and private mileage to apportion your recorded expenditure.

Expenses related to premises

You can deduct the costs of maintaining your business premises, including rent, rates, heat, light, repairs and insurance. You can also deduct the business part of these costs if you run your business from home.

Administrative costs

You can deduct the administrative costs of running your business, including advertising stationery, postage, telephone and internet. You may also be able to deduct the cost of trade or professional journals or subscriptions.

What you can and can't claim for

Allowable expenses

-⇥ Cost of goods bought for resale; cost of raw materials used; direct costs of producing goods sold; adjustments for opening and closing stock and work in progress; commissions payable; discounts given.

-⇥ Total payments made to subcontractors in the construction industry (before taking off any deductions). If you take on subcontractors in the construction industry (including work in a domestic environment, such as painting and decorating), then you probably need to register as a contractor in the Construction Industry Scheme.

-⇥ Salaries, wages, bonuses, pensions, benefits for staff or employees; agency fees, subcontracted labour costs; employer's NICs etc.

-⇥ Car and van insurance, repairs, servicing, fuel, parking, hire charges, vehicle licence fees, motoring organisation membership; train, bus, air and taxi fares; hotel room costs and meals on overnight business trips.

-⇥ Rent for business premises, business and water rates, light, heat, power, property insurance, security; use of home as office (business proportion only).

-⇥ Repairs and maintenance of business premises and equipment; renewals of small tools and items of equipment.

-⇥ Phone and fax running costs; postage, stationery, printing and small office equipment costs; computer software.

-⇥ Advertising in newspapers, directories etc., mailshots, free samples, website costs.

→ Interest on bank and other business loans; alternative finance payments.

→ Bank, overdraft and credit card charges; hire purchase interest and leasing payments; alternative finance payments.

→ Amounts included in turnover but unpaid and written off because they will not be recovered.

→ Accountant's, solicitor's, surveyor's, architect's and other professional fees; professional indemnity insurance premiums.

→ Trade or professional journals and subscriptions; other sundry business running expenses not included elsewhere; net VAT payments.

Disallowable expenses

→ Cost of goods or materials bought for private use; depreciation of equipment.

→ Own wages and drawings, pension payments or NICs; payments made for non-business work.

→ Non-business motoring costs (private use proportions); fines; costs of buying vehicles; lease rental expenses for cars with CO_2 emissions over 160g/km (15% of the amount paid); travel costs between home and business; other meals.

→ Costs of any non-business part of premises; costs of buying business premises.

→ Repairs of non-business parts of premises or equipment; costs of improving or altering premises and equipment.

→ Non-business or private use proportion of expenses; new phone, fax, computer hardware or other equipment costs.

→ Entertaining clients, suppliers and customers; hospitality at events.

→ Repayment of loans, overdrafts or finance arrangements; a proportion of interest and other charges where borrowing not used solely for the business.

→ Debts not included in turnover; debts relating to fixed assets; general bad debts.

⇢ Legal costs of buying property and large items of equipment; costs of settling tax disputes and fines for breaking the law.

⇢ Depreciation of equipment, cars etc.; losses on sales of assets (minus any profits on sales).

⇢ Payments to clubs, charities, political parties etc.; non-business part of any expenses; cost of ordinary clothing.

© Crown Copyright
Source: www.hmrc.gov.uk/worksheets/sa103f-notes.pdf

Tax relief if your business makes a loss

If your business makes a loss, you can get tax relief for it. You can do this by setting the loss against your:

⇢ other income for the same year or the previous year

⇢ gains for the same year or the previous year – if your other income is used up

⇢ other income in the previous 3 years if your business started within the past 4 years

⇢ profits from the business in later years

⇢ profits for the business in the previous 3 years if your business has ceased.

If your business made a loss in the 2008/09 or 2009/10 tax years, you can set the loss against your profits for the business in the previous three years, whether or not your business has ceased.

Getting an accountant

If you are one of those whose eyes glaze over at the very mention of tax, the best advice is to seek help. Accountants may seem an expensive luxury at first glance, but a year down the line they should prove to be money well spent. There are pros and cons to using an accountant; and while dealing with the taxman is just one of the burdens of self-employment, it is one that an accountant can alleviate. Using an agent gives you credibility. The taxman knows the agent is not going to be 'cooking the books' and may be quicker to accept the figures.

Apart from saving you a lot of headaches, a good accountant will probably save you money in unnecessary tax. They know all the allowances and legitimate expenses and will make sure you claim back all that is your right.

Reasons to get an accountant

It's your time

As a freelancer you charge an hourly rate for your time, and this is how you make money. If you are spending that time working on your accounts, it's time that you could be using to generate more income. As a non-expert the accounts are going to take you quite a bit of time, especially the first time you sit down to do them.

Accuracy

If you complete a document incorrectly then HMRC will send it back to you to do again, which could lead to you submitting it late. If you miss a deadline for tax returns, then you could face a fine. At worst, your forms could be sent to a tax inspector, who will then go through every single element of your finances with a fine-tooth comb. An accountant will get it right first time, and on time.

Tax planning

Completing the forms correctly is one thing, but are you saving the most money? A good accountant will make sure you take advantage of every legal way to minimise your tax bill. Tax laws change constantly and you are unlikely to know about every latest nuance. Why should you?

Through tax planning, your accountant will offer advice that allows you to operate in a way which gives you the biggest tax advantages. They can also give personal financial advice too, as personal and business finances are so closely linked for freelancers.

Growing the business

An accountant can be a great source of advice to help you develop your business. They can act as a business consultant and a 'sounding board', and they will come to know your business well. If you face problems at any point, they can provide advice based on their experience over the years and will usually have connections to other professionals such as bankers and lawyers, who can help you out.

Finding an accountant

Personal recommendation is always a good place to start. Ask other freelancers who they use and how happy they are with the service they receive. Look for somebody who has experience of working with freelancers and understands the specific issues they face. You may want to work with somebody who is geographically near if you feel the need to deal with them face to face.

There are also many websites that help you find an accountant, allowing you to search for a firm. Use them to create a shortlist and speak to each of them to find out what they charge and whether you feel comfortable with them. Try these:

-> www.choose-your-accountant.co.uk

-> www.find-uk-accountant.co.uk

-> www.justaccountants.co.uk.

Most will have an initial chat without charging and that should give you a feel of whether or not you are talking the same language. Whoever you choose, make sure you get on with them and can trust them implicitly. The wrong person could cost you dear.

Take advice early

Make sure you talk to an accountant before you start. It is no good waiting for the first year to come and go and then discovering a few tips that would have saved you money.

An accountant will be able to advise whether or not you are better off to launch as a limited company or to operate as a sole trader. They will also advise on partnership issues and should generally steer you in the right direction.

More advice may well be needed if you are looking for capital with which to launch your business. Your accountant may help with a business plan and suggest tax-effective ways of seeking backing.

> ### Startups Tip
> Nearly all accountants are happiest when receiving a good set of accounts on a disk. Find out what package suits them best or is compatible with your system. The taxman will take computerised tax forms too so if you are not using an accountant, this will also help in any direct dealings.

Doing without an accountant

One myth is that the taxman is an ogre out to get you at any cost. This is not true. They will come down hard on any offenders, but if you are genuine they will be as helpful as they can.

If you need help and do not have an accountant, do not be afraid to ask. Officially, the tax office says returns have to be back in during September to qualify for assistance, but if you have a simple question, phone up and ask.

Generally most tax officers would rather sort something out over the phone in a few minutes than spend days doing needless paperwork.

Invoicing

You've done the work, but before you receive payment, you will need to invoice your client. Don't worry if you haven't done it before. As with other elements of admin, the important thing is to put a system in place that works for you, and stick to it.

This is crucial to ensure that you don't run into cashflow problems. While you are waiting for payment from clients, you will have bills of your own to settle. Your customers need to understand how much they need to pay and by when. Explaining your terms clearly on your invoice will help.

An invoice is the bill you send to a client for the amount they owe you for a job done. While many clients have automated payment systems, or pay their providers with an online service, many clients still need a hard copy invoice in order to pay you.

What the invoice should include

All invoices should clearly state that this is what they are with the word 'invoice' printed clearly on them. They should also include:

-> a unique identification number to make tracking the invoice easier. This is important when it comes to chasing payments. It could include your initials or those of a client, a note of the date or year, and a number to indicate where it comes in your system; e.g INV 531/12/BBC is invoice number 531, issued in 2012 to the BBC

-> your company name, address and contact information

-> your National Insurance number and tax registration number

-> information needed to make a payment, such as your bank account details

-> the company name and address of the customer you are invoicing

-> a clear description of what you are charging for

-> the date the goods or service were provided to the client

-> the date of the invoice

-> the amount being charged, broken down into separate elements if necessary

-> VAT amount if applicable

-> the total amount owed

→ the terms of payment: how long after the invoice date you require payment. Thirty days is considered standard. You are legally entitled to charge interest on unpaid invoices to encourage organisations to pay promptly. You may wish to say on your invoices that you will charge interest on late payments to encourage prompt payment. If an invoice isn't settled within your payment terms, you can send a new invoice with interest added.

In addition, if you are a sole trader and/or VAT registered, the law requires you to provide the following additional information on any invoices you send to your customers:

→ the trader's name or any business name being used

→ an address where any legal documents can be delivered if you are using a business name.

If you are registered for VAT, you must also put the following information on your invoices:

→ the date the invoice is issued

→ your customer's name and address

→ your business name, address and VAT registration number

→ date of supply to the customer

→ a description sufficient to identify the supply of goods or services

→ the quantity of the goods or services with a unit price – excluding VAT

→ the rate of VAT per item

→ the total amount of VAT

→ amount owed without VAT added

→ the total amount owed (including VAT).

How the invoice should look

When it comes to devising your invoice template, there are free versions that you can download from the web. Microsoft Word also provides a batch of customisable business documents that look professional and save you from having to design your own, or pay for somebody else to do it. See Appendix 5 for an example invoice.

You are required to have your details on the invoice, so make it work for you by introducing some branding. This will help make you more memorable for future jobs. Include a logo and a tagline explaining what you do. Include your website address and social media details if you have them.

When it comes to the details of the job, spell it out precisely to make sure there are no misunderstandings. This can mean providing the number of hours worked plus the hourly rate, or you may want to break down the job into individual tasks with their separate charges. This also gives the client a more detailed picture of your charges, which can be useful when it comes to them commissioning future jobs as they will have a good idea of what you will charge.

Print the total in bold at the bottom of the invoice to make it easy for the accounts team to spot.

Give the invoice a good read-through to make sure all the details are correct and that there are no typos before you send it. You've gone to a lot of trouble to present a professional image with your work and demeanour so far. Don't blow it by making an elementary error on the invoice, such as spelling the client's name wrongly.

Electronic invoicing

Electronic invoicing systems are becoming more common. If you only produce the odd invoice then they're probably not necessary. However, as your business grows and becomes more complex, they could be worth considering.

There are various systems on the market, but basically they allow you to keep track of the work you have undertaken as well as your expenses. Once details are entered on to the system, an invoice is generated and sent to the client. The system then monitors payment to let you know when the money has arrived in your bank. Because there is a robust paper trail, it should make things a lot easier when it comes time to file your end of year accounts.

Each system has its own quirks and levels of support, so it's probably worth asking around to see what other people use and what they think of it. If you have an accountant, you could also ask what systems they recommend. Typically you pay a monthly fee for the service.

Some of the systems on the market include:

⇢ Crunch

⇢ Free Agent Central

⇢ Invoice2go

⇢ KashflowQuickbooks: a software package for PCs.

> **Startups Tip**
> Check out www.freshbooks.co.uk, a quick online invoicing system that allows you to create and track involves and access them from any computer.

Invoicing and payment terms

Here are some commonly used invoice payment terms and their meanings.

TABLE 4: Invoice payment terms

Net monthly account	Payment due on last day of the month following the one in which the invoice is dated
PIA	Payment in advance
Net 7	Payment seven days after invoice date
Net 10	Payment 10 days after invoice date
Net 30	Payment 30 days after invoice date
Net 60	Payment 60 days after invoice date

(Continued)

TABLE 4: Invoice payment terms

Net 90	Payment 90 days after invoice date
EOM	End of month
21 MFI	21st of the month following invoice date
1% 10 Net 30	1% discount if payment received within ten days otherwise payment 30 days after invoice date
COD	Cash on delivery
Cash account	Account conducted on a cash basis, no credit
Letter of credit	A documentary credit confirmed by a bank, often used for export
Bill of exchange	A promise to pay at a later date, usually supported by a bank
CND	Cash next delivery
CBS	Cash before shipment
CIA	Cash in advance
CWO	Cash with order
1MD	Monthly credit payment of a full month's supply
2MD	As above plus an extra calendar month
Contra	Payment from the customer offset against the value of supplies purchased from the customer
Stage payment	Payment of agreed amounts at stages

© Crown copyright 2011
Source: www.businesslink.gov.uk/bdotg/action/detail?itemId=1073791761&type=RESOURCES#

Getting paid

You've put your invoice system in place, designed a funky little logo to go on the top of it, then you send it off to the client and wait.

And wait, and wait . . .

The unfortunate thing about freelancing is that you are at the whim of those you have done work for. Your invoice may state that you would like to be paid within 30 days, thank you very much, but it can (and does) often take a lot longer.

This is one reason why it's a good idea to ensure you have some reserves built up as a freelancer. Three months of salary is good, six is even better. The last thing you want is to be so desperate for a payment to come in that you spend valuable time chasing it up when you could be doing more work. Chasing payment is dead time for you. There will be no additional money beyond what you are owed.

What to do when payment is due

When payment is due, don't be afraid to ask for it. It's your money, after all, and you have advanced somebody credit by working in advance of payment. If you've done the job right, you're entitled to be paid.

Before you do anything, check that your invoice is correct. This means making sure that it is for the correct amount and job, but also that you are submitting it in the way that the company requires. Internal accounting procedures can be confusing, so make sure that they spell out what is expected of you as a freelancer. Do you have to raise a credit note? Does the client require a hard copy invoice? Who should you direct the invoice towards? If you can't answer these questions, you may find that you won't be paid.

Any disputes or complaints that delay payment must be addressed promptly. Some customers will pay promptly while others are habitual late payers.

You will, of course, have a timetable for chasing debtors. In a small business, it could be something like this.

- → At the sale/completion of project: send out invoice.

- → 21 days: send statement reminding payment due after 30 days.

- → 30 days: if not paid, send reminder statement, restating terms and pointing out payment is overdue.

- → 45 days: send reminder.

→ 50 days: stop supplies until paid.

→ 60 days: send final reminder.

→ 90 days: assign debt to collection agency.

This is just an example. The important thing is to have a clear timetable to keep receivables under control. Of course, the above procedures should be supplemented with phone calls – one of the most effective methods of chasing debts – faxes, emails, and even visits.

Is the cheque in the post?

There may be perfectly understandable reasons why an invoice has not been paid. It's an old cliché, but it may simply be lost in the system. If this is the case, then the sooner you are on top of things the better. A first reminder may do the trick.

If you have provided an unsatisfactory service, this may be a reason to delay payment. Always try and get feedback on a job soon after you have completed it and when you are filing your invoice. If there are problems, now is the time for the client to let you know. Look to address reasonable complaints as quickly as possible.

If you can, find out who signs off the cheques before you need to harangue them for payment. It is harder for people to stonewall somebody that they actually know, rather than simply a name on an invoice.

Check that the contact details of your client are up to date. The reason you have received no response from a business may be because it has ceased trading or changed address. Reputable companies should inform you of these details, but don't take it for granted.

Be systematic and ruthless over debt collection. Chase debts at regular intervals, and keep records of any discussions or feedback you receive. Supplement letters or emails with phone calls requesting payment.

You can perhaps exert additional pressure on the company by informing the commissioner of your services that you may no longer be able to work for the company if payment problems persist. If you are a valuable freelancer, this can help release the funds. Another option is to go further up the company. It may be that an individual department manager is to blame for slack payment. Copying in an email to their boss, or boss's boss, could shock them into action.

Of course, the flip side of this, and one reason that freelancers are so loathe to rock the boat, is that you may not get any more work from the company. It's a difficult call to make. If a company is persistently late with payment, it could be an indicator of all not being well. You could be well advised to start to distance yourself from them and seek other, more reliable employers in future.

If, on the other hand, they could be lucrative clients in future, you may have to bite the bullet on a particular debt. However, beware any business that adopts a slack attitude to payment.

What to do when payment is late

Once a debt gets over 60 days overdue, you have probably exhausted all your internal resources for collecting the debts. It is therefore necessary to intervene with a third party.

Many debt collection agencies have relationships with credit reference agencies giving them leverage to collect. Of course, there is a cost, typically between 1% and 5% of the sum, depending on circumstances.

Under the Late Payment of Commercial Debts (Interest) Act 1998, a company can charge interest to its debtors on late payments. Many collectors have solicitors associated with them and can handle litigation if it is necessary to sue for a debt.

It should not be seen as a sign of weakness to pass on a debt to a collection agency. See it as an extension of your business. A new business should be equally as professional as a large company in pursuing outstanding debts.

It is important to prioritise debts, chasing the largest debts first. It is also important to establish strong relationships with major customers to ensure prompt payment.

The longer a debt is outstanding, the less likely it is to be paid.

Credit checks

You can minimise the risk of bad debts by introducing certain credit control safeguards.

If a client is new or unfamiliar to you, ask around about their payment record. Other freelancers will be able to let you know how promptly they pay. Bad payers don't remain anonymous for long in the freelance world.

If a piece of business is big enough, you could consider some form of credit vetting to give you peace of mind. You can buy a credit report on a company, but bear in mind that these are historical documents, as they are based on past filings of accounts and other information. A lot can happen to a business in 12 months. You will also have to be sure that you can understand what they are telling you about a company's credit worthiness.

When you decide to work with a client, you may wish to set a credit limit and inform them of any terms and conditions. These should be stated in your contract and on invoices.

Make sure you send invoices as soon as possible and keep an accurate record of the date of payments due.

Ultimately, if your customer persistently fails to pay, it may be appropriate to make a claim through the small claims court. You will need to be able to prove that the debt is owed. Evidence could include briefing documents, timesheets, invoices and emails acknowledging receipt of goods and service.

Get legal advice before launching any legal proceedings.

Charging for late payment

You have a statutory right to claim interest on late payment, as well as a contractual right to claim interest if your terms and conditions of payment allow.

Purchasers cannot contract out of late payment legislation – i.e. they cannot deny the supplier their right to, for example, charge statutory interest.

Should I charge interest on a late payment?

You can charge interest on all late payments. However, even if you indicate in your terms and conditions that you will charge interest on all late payments, it is up to you whether you actually do so or not.

You should address each debt on a case-by-case basis and:

- consider the relationship with the customer
- get the opinion of customer-facing staff
- assess your credit management system.

With persistent offenders, you may need to start charging interest to act as a deterrent in the future.

What rate of interest should I use?

Rates for calculating interest are called reference rates and are fixed for six-month periods. The Bank of England base rate on 31 December is used as the reference rate for debts becoming overdue between 1 January and 30 June of the following year. The rate in force on 30 June is used from 1 July to 31 December.

You can calculate the interest payable on overdue bills by taking the relevant reference rate and adding 8% again.

Alternatively, you can set a contractual rate that may be higher or lower than the statutory rate. If you set a contractual rate, the statutory rate no longer applies.

Interest should be charged on the outstanding gross amount inclusive of VAT. No VAT is chargeable on the interest itself.

Charging interest

If you don't already charge interest, you may need to:

- adapt your credit management and billing systems
- amend invoices and terms and conditions so that they state you reserve the right to charge interest – even if you don't intend to do so under normal conditions
- notify customers of your plans and check that they understand the new terms and conditions
- contact habitual late payers to discuss how they'll be affected.

Make sure invoices include an agreed payment date so customers know when interest will start being charged – let customers know if interest starts to accumulate. Your invoices should also state that you will exercise your right to claim statutory interest (at 8% over the current Bank of England base rate) and compensation for recovery costs under late payment legislation if money owed is not received by the agreed date and under the agreed credit terms.

Before charging interest, you could issue a letter stating that the payment is late and if it is not paid within, say, seven days, interest will be charged.

Present the customer with a final receipt once the interest and the original sum have been paid, outlining details of interest charged.

The BusinessLink website (www.businesslink.gov.uk) includes an interactive calculator to help you work out the amount you can charge on an unpaid debt.

To work it out yourself, follow these steps.

1. **Work out the yearly interest.** Take the amount you're claiming for and multiply it by 0.08 (8%). For example, if you were claiming for £1,000, the annual interest on this would be £80 (1000 × 0.08 = 80).
2. **Work out the daily interest.** Divide your yearly interest from step one by 365. In the example above, you would divide £80 by 365 to get the daily interest, which rounds up to 22p a day.
3. **Work out the total amount of interest.** Multiply the daily interest from step two by the number of days the debt has been owed to you. In the above example, after 50 days this would be £10.96 (50 × 0.2192).

© Crown copyright 2011

Source: www.businesslink.gov.uk/bdotg/action/detail?itemId=1073792 170&type=RESOURCES#

Tracing a debtor

If a letter is returned via Royal Mail marked 'Addressee not known' or 'No longer at this address', never assume this is actually the case. Many practised debtors simply return a letter as 'Gone away' to give themselves more time.

Start by taking the following steps.

⇁ Check your own information to see if you have made any errors on the original information. If you identify an error, reissue your invoice immediately using the correct details.

⇁ Dial telephone numbers and re-check via a directory-enquiry facility to ensure that you have the correct number.

⇁ Try a recorded delivery letter, as this may be accepted and thus confirm occupancy.

If the debtor appears to be no longer trading from the premises you have details for, then consider the following.

⇁ Contact the debtor's local Royal Mail Sorting Office, as they may have forwarding addresses, or may confirm that the subject is 'still at the address'.

⇁ If you operate in the vicinity, try to seek information from the address or from its neighbours. However, you must have due regard to the Data Protection Act 1998. In particular, do not divulge any information about a debt to non-interested parties. You are seeking general information on a 'private matter' – 'Is there a forwarding address that they know of?'

⇁ If you know any other suppliers that your customer uses, contact them to enquire if they have been notified of their change of address.

⇁ For businesses rather than individuals, use the Yellow Pages for the area of enquiry to identify, and telephone businesses/newsagents in the locality who may well know the business or have useful information on the business' status. Again, you must have due regard to the Data Protection Act when making such enquiries.

⇥ Look at the Status/Credit Reference Report you may have obtained when opening the account, as this may give you alternative addresses. In the case of a limited company, you are entitled to contact the directors, particularly the company secretary, who has an obligation to inform any interested party of the status of the limited company.

You can contact these individuals at their home address or the address lodged with Companies House, but you cannot make them individually liable for any debt. A polite question should help you establish whether, for example, the company has entered liquidation or a company voluntary arrangement.

If this is the case, you may need to seek professional advice about your rights as an unsecured creditor to a limited company.

If these efforts fail then you could seek the help of a professional collection/tracing company, who may quote costs usually from £50 to £60.

WANT TO KNOW MORE...
For further information on debt collection and tracing agents, visit the Credit Services Association at www.csa-uk.com.

Making a court claim for money

For debts of £5,000 or less then you could seek recovery through the Small Claims Court. This is a procedure operated in the County Courts to make recovery of debts simpler. In many cases the process can be started on line through the government's website: www.moneyclaim.gov.uk.

Before making a claim you must give the other party a chance to pay by sending a final warning letter.

Risks of taking court action

Taking court action can take months, and can be expensive. You may have to:

⇢ pay court fees

⇢ spend time getting your case ready

⇢ go to a hearing.

You may have to go back to court, and pay another fee, to enforce a judgment if you win but the other side won't pay. The person who owes you money may be unable to pay if they're unemployed or bankrupt, or the company has been wound up.

If you're unsure about going ahead with a claim, seek legal advice. You can get free legal help and advice from Community Legal Advice on 0845 345 4345. You can also get help from Citizens Advice.

> **Startups Tip**
> A final note on bad debts: if, having pursued all of the options you wish to take, you still have not been paid, you can write off bad debts against your taxes.

Holidays

Paid holidays are one of the benefits you forgo when you become a freelancer, but that doesn't mean that you should never have, or need, a break. Just as you should give yourself regular breaks during the day, so you will be more productive and happier for allowing yourself some holidays throughout the year.

A break can also allow you to step back from the day-to-day grind of work (yes, even free and easy freelancers feel like that sometimes) and think about the bigger picture. How is your freelance career developing? Are there areas where you could improve what you offer and earn more money? Where do you want to be in 12 months' time?

If you have family, you need to think about them too. Don't they deserve a break and the chance to spend a bit more time with you?

Making holiday plans

Like other workers, holidays for freelancers are never stress free. You can't simply switch off, because there is nobody else to take up the slack. For some clients this could be an issue, but some planning can make things easier.

First of all, make sure that you can afford it. You should have built up a buffer fund to tide you over in tough times, and the state of this will help you decide whether or not you should go on holiday. Remember, there's no holiday pay for freelancers, and you won't be earning when you are on holiday.

There will always be times of the year when it is more feasible to take time off. Speak to your clients about the time when they are least likely to need your services. Many industries have a summer lull when you can get away, but for other sectors this could be an important period. If clients have many of their own staff on holiday, it could also be the time when they are most in need of freelance cover. You don't want to be turning work away, so do your homework in advance to find out the best time to holiday.

For some freelancers, particularly those with children of school age, there may be less choice about when you take holidays. You have an even better reason to plan ahead and work holidays into your schedule.

Spread the load

If there is work in the pipeline, try to clear the decks ahead of your break. Look to shift your deadlines so that you don't have work impinging on the holiday. Spread extra work out over the weeks leading up to your holiday. Everybody expects to work a bit harder in advance of their holidays, and freelancers are no different. It will make the first drink of the holiday taste all the better.

For some freelancers, it may be possible to continue providing a level of service for clients by doing a sort of holiday swap with another freelance colleague. This could involve them manning the phones for you and perhaps taking over some of your duties so that it doesn't completely look like the 'Closed' sign is up. Make sure that clients are okay with this arrangement, and obviously only work with somebody who is trusted and capable. You could return the favour for your colleague in lieu of payment.

Give clients notice

Let your clients know as soon in advance as you can. It might be worth adding a message to your email signature a few months before you depart. This will allow you to reschedule any projects and plan around your holiday. Clients will also have holidays planned, so you need to find time when you can both get things accomplished before and after your respective breaks.

While you're away

Ideally, you don't want to be doing any work on holiday. The whole point is to recharge your batteries. However, if there is no way to avoid doing some work, or if you have to keep a check on what's going on, get some ground rules in place to ensure that you don't simply end up working the whole vacation. Find out what is acceptable to your family. You could perhaps check your emails once or twice a day, or give over one or two days to work, and no more. Decide what works best for you.

While you are away, set up an automatic email response explaining that you are on holiday and when you will be returning. If you are unlikely to be picking up emails, let people know. Include contact details for emergency enquiries. Reset your phone voicemail with the same information.

Don't forget to enjoy your holiday. One of the reasons many of us go freelance is to feel less like a wage slave. Don't simply swap one form of servitude for another. You are on holiday to relax and spend some much needed time with friends and family, so that you return to work feeling refreshed and raring to go.

What are you waiting for? Get the dates blocked off on your year planner.

Checklist

- ☑ Get organised. Don't leave admin to the last minute. Try to set aside time to do it every week.

- ☑ Group tasks, such as invoicing and adding expenses, together to make life easier.

- ☑ Introduce a simple but easy-to-understand invoicing system. You can use an online tool if you think it will make things easier.

- ☑ Stay on top of invoices and chase late payments.

- ☑ Be aware of any tax allowances you are entitled to and make the most of them.

- ☑ Mark the key dates of the tax year on your calendar or wall-planner.

- ☑ Prepare for holidays by clearing your work load and letting clients know when you will be away.

Appendix 1

Case studies

In this chapter we chat to some freelancers about their experience of setting out on their freelance career.

 In my experience

My freelance career started soon after I left university, when, as an over-educated and unemployable master's graduate, I signed up to the government's Enterprise

Name: Simon Clarke

Position: Freelance writer and lecturer in online journalism at the University for the Creative Arts in Farnham

Website: www.freelanceunbound.com

Allowance scheme in the 1980s. Like most of the newly self-employed arts graduates I knew, I became a window cleaner, followed quickly by a move up to painting and decorating.

Unlike others, however, who aspired to move quickly into full-time corporate employment, I loved it. I enjoyed the self-reliance and control over my working day and the fact that, if a client looked like they would be trouble, you could simply walk away, knowing there were a range of other jobs waiting.

I did give in and take a salaried position, but it was these insights that saved me when, stressed and overworked a couple of years later, I quit my job as deputy production editor job on a consumer magazine. Luckily, however, the magazine was happy to take me on as a full-time freelancer for several months, which made the transition to freelance life very smooth. Not long afterwards, a friend of a friend mentioned she was looking for a long-term freelance production editor to work on a marketing business magazine at Haymarket – which began more than a decade of freelancing for its various titles.

The key to successful freelancing is confidence and contacts. Most people are too scared of losing the security of full-time employment to leave jobs they dislike, but my stint up a ladder in the 1980s helped me escape that trap. Getting a long-term freelance gig at a biggish company was crucial in developing the contacts I needed to fill my freelance diary, then branch out from sub-editing to feature writing and project management. I've done a wider range of work and gained a wider range of skills than I ever would in a full-time job.

On the downside, the major problem is payment. Many, many freelancers complain about being kept waiting for months for their money, which can play havoc with household budgeting. The only solution is relentless fiscal discipline. I'm not happy unless I have at least two tax bills' worth of cash in savings, plus contingencies for car repairs and emergency dentistry.

It's also hard to earn above a certain ceiling as a freelance in publishing, especially as a torrent of free digital content eats away at the business model. You need to be more than flexible to succeed: switching to wherever the work and the money is – be it corporate writing, PR, web design or teaching. But chances are I'll never go back.

In my experience

For me, translating freelance was something I'd planned to do for a long time. My initial plan was to stay in my in-house

Name: **Philippa Hammond**
Position: **Freelance translator**
Website: **www.philippahammond.net**

translation job for about one year, save up and then launch my freelance translation business. But a year in that job passed quickly and I realised that I still had a long way to go before I felt ready to go it alone, both in terms of my skills and my ability to run a business. So I decided to set myself a new target of staying for a few more years before going freelance.

So apart from working hard, squirreling away my pennies and daydreaming about freelance freedom, what else was I doing to achieve my freelance goal? I spent a lot of evenings online researching how others were doing it, and I did regular voluntary translations in my spare time in order to hone my translation skills. I joined several groups run by professional associations such as the Institute of Translation and Interpreting (ITI) and the Chartered Institute of Linguists (CIOL), and started reading their e-group threads. I also attended more and more professional events, and I started a blog. I had been reading other translation blogs, and realised that I was gaining so much from reading about the experiences of other translators that I wanted to contribute something of my own.

Eventually, I felt the time was right to finally go freelance, but if anything I now felt even more terrified at the prospect of freelancing than before. I needed something to make me take the plunge, while also offering a security blanket. So I hatched another plan. I started attending a short teaching course – a sort of back-up plan just in case freelancing took longer than expected to get going.

After completing that course, I no longer had any excuses to put off going freelance. However, I was still seriously lacking in business skills. So I started a business skills course run by the

ITI. I also got a part-time teaching job to help pay the bills. By October 2008 (six months after going freelance), I was finding it too difficult to fit all this in with what was by then a full-time translation workload, and I felt secure enough to stop the teaching and focus on what I really wanted.

I'm sure each freelancer will have taken a different route, and the time it takes to reach a point where you're earning a decent full-time income will vary considerably depending on various factors, including sheer good luck. Hearing how other people did it is one of the best sources of inspiration, but however you do it, careful planning is one of the best routes to a successful, sustainable freelance career.

Finally, running your own business is very fulfilling but can be scary, and so crucial qualities are determination and the ability to be brave when needed.

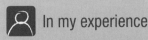

In my experience

Name: Alyson Cook

Position: Freelance PR/marketing and travel consultant

I started my new career after I hit my half-century, which coincided with being made redundant by a long-term employer. It was a shock, but the pay-off gave me the chance to assess where I wanted to go next. As a journalist, I've launched and edited many magazines, but after 20 years of major commuting, I wanted to spend more time closer to home. I also thought I could use the skills and contacts I'd gained in the past 6 years of editing a travel magazine to move into a marketing and PR role in travel, an industry which I have learnt to love.

The redundancy money gave me time to network, buy the necessary equipment and technology, speak to my contacts and pick willing brains over lunch. I've always been a 'people person' and it has paid dividends. In some ways, the offers of work came almost a little too quickly. Ideally, if I'd had more time, I could have prepared myself a little more by taking a business start-up course. I'm used to having other people doing the finance and admin and it is not my strongest area.

However, my first client, Haslemere Travel, was too good to turn down. Currently, it's the travel agency of the year, as well as being a local company that I knew well, both as a client and journalist. I am using my skills as a journalist to write news, press releases and stories for the company and its website, and my skills as a manager to link with other companies locally, nationally and abroad. I've helped the business with PR and marketing, including sponsorship and competitions, and also help organise regular speakers' lunches and events where we invite clients and partners of the business.

My business is building gradually and I'm trying to grow it organically, as I only want to work with people that I respect, like and trust. I also request that I always work on a retainer fee, so that I can manage my accounts more easily and I am convinced it builds trust (and expectations) on both sides. After Haslemere Travel another client soon came along – an award-winning Italian DMC, IC Bellagio, based in the Lake Como area.

As a freelancer, it's easy to say yes to everything out of mild panic. But I have turned down clients because I didn't know them or their business, and I also didn't want to be overstretched. I choose to work with people I want to work with. I have to believe in my clients to do my job well.

My work–life balance is a lot better now too. As the mum of a 13-year-old, I can meet her from school every day, watch her play a badminton match or read in a poetry festival. I have to plan my daily workload around this, but it's manageable. I try not to work every day in school holidays, but I am contactable. My clients know the set-up, and I am available to them.

I do occasionally miss the buzz and camaraderie of office life. There are times when it would be great to head out for a glass of wine with a colleague. When freelancing works well, there's nothing like it, but you are on your own a lot. It's tough when things go wrong (especially on the IT side!), or you have no one to bounce ideas off. Husbands will only take so much . . .!

I set up a business, rather than just registering as self-employed. I was advised to do this as it will make things easier in future if the business is scalable and I find myself employing others. It also projects a more professional image, which is something I'm very conscious of. People take you more seriously as a business, rather than a one-woman band.

My biggest problem is the pressure I put myself under. I tend to over-deliver by working too hard, because I'm eager to do a good job. Because I work from home, the client doesn't know what I have done to make something happen. A lot of the work may be speculative, or take a long time to deliver, so you feel like you have to have something to show.

I got one of my clients on a radio spot recently, but it took six months of effort before it happened. My selling skills have definitely improved!

Sometimes I think I should have made this move years ago, but I wouldn't have had the seniority at the time. I'm older and wiser, I can project that this is a serious undertaking for me and that I won't be here today and gone tomorrow. But I make sure it's plenty of fun too!

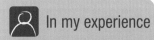 In my experience

I worked full-time in healthcare PR for nearly 10 years having, like many, landed in

Name: Nick Stewart
Position: Freelance PR consultant

the industry almost by accident. My first jobs at the Science Museum and Cancer Research UK proved excellent ways to use the communications skills I developed during my master's degree in science communication, and my more recent work with pharmaceutical companies enabled me to dust off knowledge from my biology degree.

I recently went freelance and am using short-term contracts at agencies as a way of paying the bills while I study psychology with the Open University. Freelancing is proving a brilliant way to earn good, regular money while I flirt with a new direction in my career.

My experience in a specialist area of PR has proved an advantage: there is demand for my skills, and I can charge a higher daily rate than I would otherwise be able to. One advantage of working in PR I hadn't anticipated was the predominance of women working in the industry. At my level of account director, many employees are of child-bearing age, creating a steady demand for maternity cover.

Working in a small industry increases the value of networking. All of the contracts I have been offered to date have been from people I know or have been introduced to by friends or old colleagues, and I have so far managed to avoid using recruitment consultants to find work. Cutting out the middleman has financial advantages for both you and your employers. That said, I have made friends with a number of recruiters as the market may change.

In an industry where everyone knows everyone, you do have to take care to guard your reputation. It is a cliché, but you really are only as good as your last piece of work. Potential employers are likely to recognise the name of at least one employer on your CV and won't hesitate to ask their opinion.

Social media is proving very useful for networking. I have had a number of approaches through LinkedIn, even without actively managing my profile or using advanced features such as recommendations. Recruiters use the website to find out who is available. They can also see who you know in common as a means of finding out very quickly whether you're good or not.

Facebook is also useful. I am friends with other freelancers and, because there is a steady supply of work at the moment, we refer jobs to each other, which has been fantastic. Employers are desperate to avoid the fees charged by recruitment consultants and appreciate being able to find new freelancers using trusted recommendations.

In my experience

I was a reluctant and unwilling candidate for a freelance life. I had worked as an independent freelance consultant for seven years, but when a great job in a large corporate setting was

Name: Sally Gritten

Position: President, Centre for Human Systems Dynamics (UK), freelance consultant

Website: www.gritten.co.uk; www.hsdinstitute.org

offered, I jumped at it. Here at last was security, status and a good income. And I assumed I would stay in that role until retirement saw me out. But, that was not to be.

Many years into the job, I got sick. Not so sick that I was going to die, but sick enough that the 60-hour weeks, managing 30 people and living with the stress of a floundering economy became untenable. Added to that, my illness requires a lot of management and treatment time and can unexpectedly land me in hospital.

Before my illness, I lived with a common illusion that I could plan my future. Millions of people employed in the private and public sector, thousands of graduates and untold numbers of young people believed that, too. Then the bottom fell out of the economy and, like me, they were all faced with a future they could neither predict nor control. For me, that reality became the bedrock of my work as a teacher, public speaker, consultant and coach. Now, 5 years on, I wouldn't consider any other career except one that is freelance.

That is not to say that I don't worry about where the next client will come from, or have 'good' months and 'bad' months when it comes to income. It would also be fair to say that I love working at my computer until 12pm in my pyjamas. And, crucially important, I love the work I do and the clients I work with.

But those are not the things that make me a person who wants a freelance life. What really makes the difference is that I know

now that there is no position, no role, and no job – PAYE or freelance – that can take away the uncertainty in which we all live. So given that uncertainty is certain, being freelance allows me to embrace that uncertainty rather than deny it.

I didn't know this when I started my freelance career, but not being confined to a corporate job meant I could pursue other things. I needed to work to live, and I did, taking anything I could get as a freelancer. But I also began to study complexity theory and, through human systems dynamics, I am learning to understand that our ability to shape the future lies within the boundaries of influencing conditions, watching for patterns, learning how to shift less than useful patterns and applying adaptive action to my career. I actively practise mindfulness and try to stay in the here and now without judgement (not always successfully, I might add.)

That is where I am today. Tomorrow could be different – or not. Right now a freelance life gives me the opportunity to practise living with uncertainty. It isn't always easy, but it is always interesting.

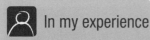

In my experience

Name: Annalise Rickman

Position: Freelance event director

My degree is in journalism and, after graduating, I worked in TV production for 2 years in Zimbabwe. I wanted to become an editor, but it became clear that this wasn't going to happen, so I had to reassess where my skills lay. I stumbled across a job in C&I (conference and incentive travel) without really knowing what it was, but it sounded like fun. I worked for a destination management company in Zimbabwe called Green Route, managing inbound programmes for 3 years.

Eventually I reached the stage where I wanted to travel and go to the UK, but I found it difficult to get a position due to my Zimbabwean passport, which made it awkward to travel. So I started freelancing and did absolutely anything, no matter how hard or mind-numbing. As a result, I gained a lot of experience that people who took a different career route don't have. When I naturalised and the visa issue went away, I went straight into an account manager role and moved on to become an event director within about 5 years.

I think there are three types of event freelancer.

1. Those who prefer working on-site and who are not equipped or prepared to be behind a desk all day.
2. Those who only work in the office. Many women with children do this because it is more predictable and does not require travel, which is a big part of this business.
3. Then there are people like me who are open to any kind of event work. It makes it easier to find work because we are more flexible.

Having said that, I tend to seek out contract work, as the freelance life is quite precarious financially. I've mostly done maternity cover where you know that you can be guaranteed at least six months work, which provides a degree of security.

Some people start freelancing in events when they are older and more experienced. At that stage, it can become almost a lifestyle choice. For me, the decision to go freelance was taken for me when my last company, THA, went bust in 2008 and the recession hit the events industry hard, making it difficult to find good work.

At the time I needed work quickly, so put out a few emails and quickly got a freelance job offer back. I've been doing it ever since and it becomes easier to get the next job because you are networking all the time and freelance colleagues pass on information about jobs.

I have also used recruitment agencies. Whilst many creative agencies tend to avoid using recruitment agencies for freelance roles, corporate clients seem to use them when they need to get hold of somebody at quite short notice and they simply don't have the time or resources to find somebody themselves, so it is worth being on the books of agencies, in my experience.

My last contract needed somebody who was quite experienced, quickly and they didn't have time to risk recruiting from an online job board. If you have a huge contract come in, you need somebody who is vouched for, which is what recruitment agencies do.

Other useful tools are things like LinkedIn and (in my industry) a site called FreeSource (www.freesourceuk.com), which is a database of event freelancers. Job boards have been slightly less useful as you get people putting up projects at silly rates.

I have worked with agencies, event management companies and corporates, so I have a varied experience. I could get another full-time job, but freelancing suits my private life, as my husband and step-child live in Toronto and I need to take regular time off to see them. The standard 25 days isn't enough, but freelancing allows me the freedom to do this.

There are also downsides to freelancing that you have to bear in mind. Usually, you are not hired to do an easy project. Freelancers are brought in when there is a lot of work on, or a particularly tough project that an organisation has to skill up for. You are a fixer or a trouble-shooter, and because you are getting a good daily rate, they want to maximise their investment. There are usually incredibly tight deadlines in place which can pile pressure on to the freelancer.

You can also inherit situations not of your making, such as where somebody has over-promised to a client and expects you to deliver. Personally, I'd never blame a freelancer if I had hired them, but in some companies, the buck stops with the freelancer.

A good freelancer needs a mix of skills, especially diplomacy. If you are more experienced than the people you are working with, sometimes you have to take a back seat and not offer advice unless asked for it. Sometimes it's better to bite your lip and deal with a problem once it has happened, even if that seems illogical.

Reliability is obviously essential, but you don't want to be somebody who just turns up and takes the money. Enthusiasm is important too. And you need to be (where possible!) calm and graceful under pressure and have an ability to get on with everybody from the VIP to the hotel porters.

As a freelancer, you're only as good as your last job.

In my experience

Name: Melanie May
Position: Freelance writer

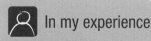

My decision to go freelance was really about me being able to have my cake and eat it. I had a child who I wanted to look after myself rather than put into childcare, and I also wanted, and needed, to work.

Four years down the line, I would say that on balance it has worked, but it hasn't been easy. Working at home with a small child in tow is a challenge. For one, small children tend not to respect 'work time' and there is only a certain amount one can do in the evenings when they're in bed. Working around them can be very difficult, even if you're in another room. I have lost count of the telephone calls interrupted by sudden demands that just won't wait, or just by very loud screaming. Luckily, as a journalist and copywriter, I only ever talk to nice people who don't appear to mind.

Crucially, I also had my partner at home most of the time when my daughter was really small, which enabled me to work during the daytime when I needed to. Had this not been the case, I would have needed some sort of childcare for her, which would rather have defeated the object of me going freelance in the first place. Children are very demanding, and the cosy image I had of her sleeping peacefully next to me while I worked never quite translated into reality.

Since she's been old enough for pre-school and (now) primary school, I've been able to take on more work to fill the hours she is out of the house. However, making this work demands focus. When possible I only schedule phone interviews within school hours, and on occasion I have to turn down work because it doesn't fit in with school holidays and my daughter is not yet old enough or willing to entertain herself for hours on end.

What I've learned is that working from home with a small child in tow is possible, but only if you can be flexible about when you work, and then very focused during those work hours. Because it is difficult to work anywhere near full-time hours, it can also be a struggle financially; but balance that with the very precious time it gives you with your child, and I think it is well worth it.

In my experience

Finding work is the biggest challenge any freelancer faces. I was fortunate

Name: Nick Martindale

Position: Freelance journalist

enough to be able to take a decent proportion of my old job with me; this won't be an option for everyone but it's certainly worth exploring.

Building up a regular client base is a slow but steady process, and is preferable to working for just two or three clients. My experience is that it gets easier the longer you've been at it. Initially, you won't have the same breadth of experience as other freelancers, so your best prospects are likely to be those contacts you already have, whether former employers, ex-colleagues or even people you trained with many years ago.

Get back in touch with contacts (preferably before you leave your job), build up a strong network on LinkedIn and let as many people as possible know you'll be available to take on freelance work.

Once you've picked up a few jobs, you'll be in a much stronger position to pitch people cold. Find out who makes the decisions at companies where you'd be a good fit – in my case magazines or newspapers covering topics on which I could demonstrate some previous experience – and send them a brief introductory note outlining your credentials.

Make sure you tailor each pitch individually to that business – it's easy to spot those which have been sent out en masse – and make it as relevant as you can. They don't want your life story and you may need to omit parts of your background if they're not a close fit. Back this up with examples of your work. I normally refer people to my LinkedIn profile, where they can find out more and access a few references. In the longer term, a dedicated website could perform a similar role. If you don't hear back, follow up in a week or two.

Finally, let people know subtly — perhaps through an email footer — that you're freelancing, and once you've built up a good relationship don't be afraid to mention this directly. Much of my copywriting work has come from people I've interviewed somewhere down the line and who are looking for a writer who understands their particular industry.

You need to prepare yourself, too, for the ups and downs that are an inevitable part of freelancing. Being methodically organised should help you cope with peak periods, and while it's never good to turn down work, there are times when it's unavoidable. But there will be downtime too, and that's when you can concentrate on trying to build up your client base.

In my experience

The brief for any design project is absolutely vital. It forms the starting point

Name: Tracey Goodland
Position: Freelance designer

of the work and everything comes from it. It is important to get the details correct and also to make sure both client and designer are fully aware of what they are getting and what they need to do.

Particular, with a new client, I like to have them fill out a brief sheet for me. It not only informs me as to what they want but also gives them a chance to think it through from a design perspective. It can highlight things they haven't considered previously and bring to light any potential problems.

I haven't really had any disagreements with clients regarding what they wanted and what I provided, and I think this is because I always have a thorough briefing discussion with them prior to starting any work. With experience, I have come to have a good understanding of what a client is looking for even if they can't really express it. If there are issues with a project, then I will discuss them with the client and come to some agreement on how to proceed. Otherwise, I would generally end up doing more work – so it is in my interest to get the brief right before I start, so as not to end up with extra unpaid work.

I went freelance about 3 years ago, as I was made redundant from my full-time employment. I had a one-year-old child at home and felt it would be good to work from home. I had several clients established from my full-time work and I started from this base. I also had some redundancy money to fall back on if I needed it, so I had some security.

Part of setting up was doing a lot of research into how other designers and agencies work – I also used my own work experiences. We always had a detailed brief sheet and I discovered that all agencies do too. They also have terms and conditions, and I wanted to follow this example and establish myself as a professional agency rather than a one-man band freelancer.

I used elements from my research to construct the brief sheet and terms and conditions. It is important to note that the terms and conditions are not legal – they are my business guidelines really. If a client reads these (they are attached to all quotes and are available on my website), they have a good idea of what they can expect from me and my business.

I guess that both the terms and conditions and the brief sheet give both the client and the designer a good understanding of what each other is about, before either make any commitment.

[NB See Appendix 3 for an example of a brief sheet and Appendix 4 for example terms and conditions.]

In my experience

I was working for a big multinational on a nine-month contract and the opportunity of a full-time job came up, but I really

Name: Rob Clayton
Position: Freelance photographer
Website: www.robclayton.co.uk

wanted to go freelance, and my boss at the time said that they would be able to put some work my way. Although I had worked for a commercial photographer, it was still quite early days in my career. To pursue a career in creative photography I decided to go freelance. It was an instinctive thing. I knew a couple of photographers and they encouraged me to go this way.

It was a risk, but a calculated one. I was single, but I had a mortgage to pay. Working with the photographer had given me an insight into the business side of photography. The work from my old employer gave me about 50% of what I worked out I needed to earn a month to survive. For the rest, I had ideas of how to market myself, and I worked hard at approaching some old clients and local businesses in Wembley, the area I lived in at the time. I got some work from the local authority.

Some people see freelancing as being this great freedom, but for me it was the opposite. I come from a background where pennies have to be watched and I was a bit cautious about how I built the business. I always knew how much I had in the bank and how much I was owed.

I got an accountant before I went freelance, and he gave me some very good advice on keeping track of my income and outgoings. It was a very simple thing, but great discipline. In the first year I tracked everything I spent on a weekly basis. My degree had also had a business module as well, so I knew how to do cash flow forecasts. I was absolutely dedicated to making a go of freelancing, and even had a back-up plan of driving a minicab if I needed to make ends meet. Fear of failure was a big spur for me.

My portfolio of work was quite strong from the off and that helped open doors. I'm quite confident; if I can get in front of somebody, I can convert that meeting into work. It's all about confidence and selling yourself. Those skills have definitely got better as I have developed my career.

At first I didn't aim too high with my aspirations. It was fairly bread and butter stuff – not at all glamorous – to help me establish myself, but it has all led on to other things. I did better than I thought I would in the first year, so I didn't have to drive a minicab.

At certain times throughout my career I have looked to up my game and get better work. I've had to think quite creatively. For example, to get more corporate work, which is better paying, I would go through the *Guardian*'s media section on Monday looking to see who was recruiting picture editors or marketing managers. After a few months, I would contact those companies knowing that they had new people in place and look to see if I could present my portfolio. Occasionally it would lead to appointments where I would generally convert the work. Nothing beats a well-targeted cold call but you have to have the confidence to convert it.

At other stages where I felt my work was stalling I've tried to up my game and get more magazine work, which was more creative. I started working for Haymarket Publishing in 1999 and have done more than 400 shoots for them now. This allowed me to approach other magazine companies and my income stepped up accordingly.

As a freelancer, you have to be aware that work could dry up from a client at any time. Your contact may move on, they may want a different style, or they may be cutting back. You have to be constantly alert to new opportunities.

In photography you have to decide whether you want to be an operator, providing pictures that are not that distinctive, such as school photos or wedding shoots, or a creative photographer.

I always look to add value in my work, whether it's through my relationship with the client and the ease of working with them or through adding new skills to my portfolio. Recently I've been looking at improving my own photographic techniques. You can never stand still in this business. By looking at the work of other photographers, I've been inspired again, and it has given me new ideas.

The next step for me is to do more work in the design and advertising world. It's another step up and it's the sort of progression I'm always aiming for.

A creative freelance needs to enjoy what they do. It's a vocation. But it also pays back depending on how much effort you put into your career.

In my experience

My corporate communications degree led to an interest in marketing, in which I did a master's. This in turn led to a full-time job in qualitative research. It was a fascinating job, travelling

Name: Natasha Curnock

Position: Freelance researcher and psychotherapist

Website: thepsychotherapygroup. co.uk/natasha.aspx

around the world and looking at the way that people responded to brands in different cultures. I loved being involved in helping brands and organisations change strategic direction.

It was also exhausting, and after a few years I began to think about retraining to do something else. I was looking for a career that was more meaningful and allowed me to get more involved with people. As a researcher you tend to meet people for a short time while interviewing them, but never learn more about their lives. I was also tiring of the usual aspects of office politics.

I decided to train as a psychotherapist. It was an undertaking that I knew would be demanding, so I decided to quit my job and throw myself into training full time. I thought that I could focus and do the course in 2 years and be ready to practise. However, once I started, it became clear that it wasn't as simple as that. My course involves a lot of self-development and it is not really time-bound. After the initial first year of training, it could take as long or short a time as you wanted. And I came to realise that not everything had to be done in the quickest time possible.

Before starting the course I didn't really know anything about freelancing. My previous company didn't use freelancers, but through speaking to others on the course, it became clear that many had portfolio careers and were using their existing careers to get them through their training.

After a year the training was less intensive, so I picked up contracts to work and did my courses in the evenings. I started to get calls from old colleagues asking about my availability and decided that it made sense to work on a freelance basis. It was surprising to find that people would pay me a day rate to work for them.

Qualitative research is relatively flexible, so I was able to work around my studies. I also found that by approaching research agencies and client companies I was able to drum up enough work. This was hardly surprising, as my rates at the time were quite low. They probably couldn't believe their luck.

Balancing freelance research work and my studies, and eventually my practice, has been a process of trial and error. In the early days I would only have two or three clients a day but would have to give up a full day's pay from research. I love psychotherapy, but in the short-term at least, it doesn't pay all my bills. Research work is much more lucrative, so I've tried to arrive at a situation where I allocate certain days to each career.

However, even that is an evolving process. I used to set aside Mondays, Tuesdays and Fridays for research work, but a colleague eventually pointed out that there wasn't much research fieldwork on Fridays so I was able to devote it to therapy. Clients tend to want to see you in the evenings, but then I found I wasn't happy working Friday evenings. So now I don't see clients then. Balancing my workload is a work in progress.

For now, my two careers will continue to go along on parallel tracks. There are aspects of both that I like and dislike. I'm lucky in that sense. I met people training as therapists because they hated their jobs in IT or management consultancy, for example.

Building a therapy practice is a long and slow process. You need to get known so people refer clients to you and existing clients recommend you. I have been doing research longer so it is easier to pick up regular, relatively well-paid work.

The two jobs are complementary in the sense that they both require you to be open and sociable. You can't go into them if you are introverted. Running research focus groups has helped, in the sense that I am used to speaking to strangers and putting them at their ease. I'm also used to working in a pressurised environment, so if therapy clients come to me with work-related issues I can appreciate what they are going through.

In my experience

I always knew that I wanted to start my own business at some point. My late father had his own company so I've always been commercially aware.

Name: Adam Baggs

Position: Managing director of Soaring World PR

I started working for an events agency as an events manager, writing proposals for corporate events for companies like Citroen. Writing was something I really liked and I wanted to focus on, but I wasn't really sure how to do it. I had an interview with a PR agency which initially didn't seem right, as I knew nothing about PR. However the agency was really keen on moving into events so it was a great fit. They taught me the ropes of PR and I brought my events background to them.

After a couple of great years there, I moved to another business where things didn't quite work out. I was unhappy there and the experience probably crystallised the feeling that I wanted to work for myself. At that point there was a fortuitous stroke of luck. I was about to go on holiday for a week when I got a call from an old contact at an events agency, wanting to know if I knew anybody who could do some freelance writing for them. Instead of going on holiday I spent the week working for them and devising a business plan for my start-up.

When I went into work the next week I told them I was leaving. I was in the fortunate position of being fairly indispensable to them, so I was able to leave with a few days a week guaranteed work from them. I was up and running as a PR agency, and fairly soon I landed another client.

The real break came after about eight months when we landed the contract to handle the Barbican's events PR. After winning a contract of that stature and size, we've never looked back. The feedback they gave me was that they liked the size that we were at, as it would give them a more personal service.

Right from the time we started as a company, I knew that I wanted the business to grow, although at the start it was just me freelancing. However, I set it up as a limited company, so the mindset was always that it would grow into something bigger. By having the company financially and legally set up, I knew that we were always heading towards it. The desire and drive was always to take it on.

Even in the early days I never presented the company as just me, but as a real business. However, as a small, boutique agency, you can lose out on some pieces of business if the client is worried that they will represent too much of your business. You have to achieve a certain scale to get some pieces of business.

I still work across all the accounts, but I'm now involved at a more strategic level. I have to be careful how I spend my time, as it just isn't worthwhile for me to be doing things like updating websites, sending out cuttings reports and ordering the stationery – all things that I had to do when we were growing. One of the best hires we have made was not a PR person but an office administrator, who took so much off my shoulders and allowed me to focus on strategically important aspects of the business. The difference she made was quite astonishing.

We have scaled the business up organically. We work with a lot of partners, including freelancers. As the business expanded, we had to make the call about whether we would bring another freelancer on board, or whether it was worth hiring people to work for us full time. In the end we did take someone on, growing the business in line with a strategic business plan and client wins.

Our targets have been realistic, and we have grown the business through profits without having to take external investment. We have had to spend quite heavily on some things, such as technology to allow remote working. We have clients in Japan and in other countries, so I can be on the road a bit.

As the business owner, you have to have a more rounded set of skills, or your business plateaus. You only ever react to the business rather than thinking in a more strategic manner, and you'll only get so far. A big growth challenge is identifying skill gaps and when it makes sense to fill them. You have to start thinking about the right people to bring in and at what point. For example, I could have produced our website, but it reached a point where it was no longer a valid use of my time. When that happens, you have to assess what resources you need to move the business forward. It's a big change from being a freelancer, where you try to keep your investment as low as possible and to do as much as you can yourself.

Financial savvy is something that is very important. You don't need to be doing your own bookkeeping, but you should know how to read the key metrics on your balance sheet and recognise what they are telling you about the state of the business. It's criminal if you don't.

As a freelancer, you can get very excited in the early days when it appears that you are earning more money than you did on staff. But you have to be able to think beyond the current contract. The economic downturn brought this home to us, as we had to seriously consider what might happen if we lost clients. It forced us to think creatively about different ways that we could work for some clients. Ultimately it was better than losing business altogether, but it was something that a freelancer would have struggled to do. You don't have that flexibility.

By thinking strategically in this way we have actually been able to grow.

Having systems in place is another important thing that marks out a business from a sole trader. We do have set processes that allow the business to run smoothly. It's not all in my head where other members of staff can't access it. It also means that everything that comes out of the agency has a consistent quality.

We have now been going for 5 years and we have doubled financially year on year. A few years ago we had a business consultant in to help us revisit our business plan. As an exercise it was useful in focusing us on the financials, the ethos of the business and what we wanted to achieve, even if the resulting document was a bit unwieldy.

I'm also lucky in the business I'm in that I get to speak to a lot of senior business people about their businesses. I've picked up some great pieces of wisdom from chief executives and MDs.

The challenge of running my own business is something that I love. People sometimes say that it's a brave thing to do, but we have clients on 2 year contracts. Who has that sort of security in their job?

There are great highs and lows, and things can turn round on a sixpence, but I wouldn't change it.

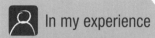 In my experience

You cannot survive as a freelancer unless you expand your portfolio of skills.

Name: Mike Fletcher
Position: Freelance journalist

In my experience, after 7 years editing two magazines and developing a web strategy with my previous company, I was ready for a change. Developing the web strategy had excited me about the possibilities for online journalism, but also frustrated me as I realised that what the company was prepared to do was far removed from what was possible. I concluded that I could learn more about online journalism if I left my old job.

It was also a natural break, as the company wanted to merge the two magazines and I didn't feel that it was something I wanted to do. My interests lay elsewhere and it was the catalyst for me moving on.

As an editor, the further up the ladder you are, the further away from writing you become. You start to head down the publisher route with budgets and staff issues. But I had trained as a writer and that's what I am happiest doing, as well as what I wanted to go back to doing.

It's quite a big, scary decision to go freelance. You obviously wonder if you will get enough work. By diversifying into new areas I hoped that I would make it work for me.

My original strategy as a freelancer had been to move away from specialism towards the consumer magazine market. I pitched ideas, but you cannot make a good living because they commission six months in advance. It's a slow process and you have to build in other things.

I specialise in event and business tourism and soon realised that this is where I should concentrate my efforts. I started to look at the opportunities for online journalism with social media in particular. By spending time on the London tech scene, it became apparent that the events sector did not yet know how to make use of the technology. So I became a social media consultant to the sector as well as an online journalist.

Digital media is a fast developing area, but I always felt that if I knew more about it than the next person, then I could stay one step ahead. You have to keep developing yourself and learn what's new. It's a lot easier when you are not in a large corporation. You pick things up a lot quicker when you are on your own.

I started to pick up social media contracts, such as running Facebook and Twitter accounts for various clients. At one point I had about seven Twitter accounts going at the same time. Individually they don't earn you a fortune, but it's surprising how they mount up.

London 2012 was something I also wanted to be involved with, so I targeted London & Partners, formerly known as Visit London, the city's tourism convention bureau. I pitched to them and got a one day a week retainer to write their website copy and news about events. I also put together a social media strategy and worked my way into writing guides for them. For London 2012 I am a contributing editor for the Olympics London Media Centre.

You have to be in a position to make things happen as a freelancer. Networking is more important than it ever has been, especially if you are trying to freelance in your previous industry. People forget you very quickly.

I had to rebuild myself as media neutral. People can associate you with a certain publisher, and it can hamper your ability to get work from other companies. I joined the board of the International Special Events Society (ISES) in a voluntary capacity as the VP of communications. Working for an industry body was part of my personal rebranding process to position myself as an events industry expert.

In my first year I almost ran myself into the ground. In the second year I realised I couldn't keep that up. I slowed down, became more selective in the work I accepted and started to charge a bit more. You shouldn't be afraid to charge what you think you are worth. As a result I had a better standard of life and earned more by finding the right balance of projects.

Sadly, there have been a lot of redundancies in the events sector, but it has been to my benefit as it has opened up opportunities for freelancers. You have a lot of conversations about projects but only about half come off. I'm getting better at spotting what's a conversation and what's work.

Photography is another string to my bow which I've been developing. You can never stand still as a freelancer. You've got to keep looking for new areas where you can pick up work.

In my experience

Name: Roxanne Clark

Position: Freelance communications consultant

I am reassured when I look back, at those first days and weeks of working as a freelance communications consultant, that I faced the uncertainty and kept going.

At the time, I didn't feel like I had much choice. The work I was doing previously dried up suddenly and I had to call upon other skills – little did I know that my background as a newspaper journalist would provide me with such a strong foundation for the comms portfolio I have since developed for a diverse client base.

That and the threads that have run through all my contracts – tenacity, goodwill, and the 'can-do' attitude with which I meet every opportunity.

I am not saying it is easy – tenacity helps a lot when everything feels overwhelming – but I did want something different and was prepared to take risks. I also did not want the alternative, working as an employee. So, I kept on going and everything that has been thrown my way I have caught and managed to make work.

To have interests outside my specialist skills has also been essential; I was a yoga teacher and am actively involved on a charity committee, both of which have opened several windows and kept me interested.

Having worked as a journalist, I had learnt to think outside the box and meet tight deadlines as well as be endlessly curious. Diplomatic skills also go a long way to ensure clients listen to and understand the pivotal role that communications can play in setting the right tone and positioning. Moreover, in an increasingly competitive and restricted marketplace, it really is the attitude with which you approach each new contract, or bid, that will enable you to build a solid and strong portfolio.

Since those first scary and heady days 10 years ago, I have worked across the corporate, public and third sectors and turned my newspaper journalist skills into myriad roles.

Since then I have written two columns for *The Times* on stress management for teachers and office workers, established an in-house communications function in an FE college, developed and established internal communications functions and channels in two different organisations, and written the content and developed intranet based magazines. I have worked as a corporate brand consultant, repositioning the company's identity; been a news and web editor for a charity and co-edited the first contemporary UK report into women's philanthropy. Currently, I am in a central government communications role and working across both external and internal programmes and discovering skills I did not know I had.

In my experience

I got into PR after I completed a PR degree that included a placement year; I knew that having work

Name: Susie Taylor
Position: Freelance PR consultant

experience was going to get me my first job. As soon as I graduated, I was recommended for my initial consumer agency role by a journalist I had worked with during my placement year. I went for the interview and was offered the job. I then went on to join another London agency, in order to broaden my experience working across consumer, business-to-business, and corporate accounts. I then went in-house, working for a Home Office department. My goal from the start was to get as wide a range of PR experience as possible.

My first freelancing contract was through a PR recruitment agency, but now I get all my work through recommendations. At the moment my work is a mix of having my own clients and working with agencies on theirs. I want to build up my portfolio of retained clients this year whilst continuing to work with agencies. My retained clients employ me for a certain number of hours a month. I then fill the remaining time with agency contracts.

When I started, I asked a freelancing friend what he was charging, as he was at a similar level to me. My day rate varies depending on the complexity of the role, location of the job, and the duration of the assignment. I offer the same service as a PR agency (media relations, copywriting, event management, analyst outreach etc.). If I need other specialist support, then I call on other freelancer colleagues to deliver this.

Working with freelancers gives companies the opportunity to try out PR without being tied into the lengthy contract period that agencies require. Freelancers are more cost-effective because they have lower overheads than agencies. A further benefit for a client using freelancers is that they will probably get a more experienced PR since agencies usually give the day-to-day work to more junior staff.

One of the challenges of being a freelancer is working with different teams and companies all of the time. You need to be prepared to get stuck in quickly and immerse yourself in their world. Being a freelancer is great, as you don't get too bogged down with politics and you can focus on delivering great results.

Appendix 2

Example press release

PRESS RELEASE/NEWS RELEASE

YOUR LOGO

Headline: NEW GUIDE AIMS TO REVEAL THE SECRETS OF YOUR BOOK

London, 2 September 2012: A new book promises to help would-be freelancers break into the competitive world of working for yourself.

Your Book by Anon, a freelancer of more than 10 years, is a practical guide to all aspects of starting and developing your own career.

Topics covered include:

- Making the decision to go it alone
- How to set up your business
- Getting work
- Pricing your work
- Case studies of the most popular solo careers
- And much more

The author, Anon, said: 'More and more people are turning to solo careers, either through choice or necessity. It can be a great way to work for many people, but there is a lot to learn. You really do have to become a jack of all trades to make a success of it. Whether it's learning how to market yourself, improving your networking skills, or getting on top of the financial aspects of working alone, *Your Book* offers practical and hard-learned advice from real freelancers. It is the sort of book that I wish I had read when I started out.'

Your Book is published by A Publisher on 3 September 2012 and costs £9.99.

ENDS

For more information, contact Jane Doe at A Publisher:
Tel: 020 1234 1234
Email: info@apublisher.co.uk
Web: www.apublisher.co.uk

ABOUT A PUBLISHING
Set up in 2007, A Publisher is an ambitious and fast-growing publisher specialising in quality non-fiction titles that improve the way you live. We mean to be different from other publishers in a number of ways, not only with the subjects we publish in, but also by going to the heart of how each book is created, from its planning and research to its writing and design. This comes from a belief that books can deliver more than they often do.

t 020 1234 1234 | **f** 020 1234 1235 | www.yourwebsite.co.uk
Your House, Your Road, Your Town, Your City, AB1 2CD

Appendix 3

Example brief sheet

t 020 1234 1234 | **f** 020 1234 1235 | www.yourwebsite.co.uk
Your House, Your Road, Your Town, Your City, AB1 2CD

YOUR LOGO

Please fill in the following briefsheet. Your answers will help the designer to understand the requirements for your project and therefore produce the best end product for you. Please be as detailed and accurate as possible and be aware that changing the brief at a later date can affect deadlines and specifications.

About the client *Please give details of the person the designer can deal with directly on the project.*

Name
Contact details

About the project

Briefing date
Project name
Description and objective?
Is the project to be used as part of a suite of materials?
Where will the project be used/displayed?
Target audience?
Feel of the project? *Some descriptive words about the mood you want to create with the project and what your target audience should feel on seeing it.*

Project specifications

Deliverables? *(leaflet, poster etc)*
Size? *(A4, DL etc)*
Colour? *(1 colour, full colour etc)*
Pages?
Print quantity?
Print organisation required? YES NO *Further details will be required and the designer will contact you to discuss. Printing normally takes 1-2 weeks.*
Deadline for finished materials?

Other considerations *Please give details of what the designer will receive from you to work with.*

Copy? *Please supply all copy required for the project; where possible, this should be signed off by relevant persons prior to design commencing.*
Photography? *Please supply all photography required for the project OR specify photographic requirements here.*
Logos etc? *Please supply all other material to be included in the final project such as logos, signatures etc and give details here.*
Other imagery? *Do you require illustrative design solutions? Please give details here.*

Please post the finished form to Your Name, Your House, Your Road, Your Town, Your City, AB1 2CD or fill in using Adobe Acrobat and email to yourname@youremail.co.uk.

Appendix 4

Example terms and conditions

YOUR LOGO

Terms and Conditions

Costs are valid for 30 days from date of quotation. If the work quoted for is not undertaken within 30 days, a revised quotation may be supplied to the client.

Work detailed in the quotation will be undertaken by Your Logo Ltd for the quoted price, once the client has given written approval.

Any additional work (eg: amends beyond the scope of the quotation) will be agreed between Your Logo Ltd and client prior to additional work being undertaken.

Additional costs will be applied where external suppliers (eg: photography, printing) are used. This will be discussed and agreed with the client prior to any external suppliers being used.

Changes to the work agreed, originating from the client, may result in additional charges (eg: client delays, alterations to approved work). Any additional costs will be agreed with the client prior to work being undertaken.

A full breakdown of all original and additional costs can be provided to the client on request.

All accounts should be settled within 30 days of the date on the invoice.

All invoices are considered correct unless Your Logo Ltd is notified by the client within 7 days of date on invoice.

Upon cancellation of a project already undertaken, a reasonable payment for work carried out will be charged where appropriate.

The copyright of all work originated by Your Logo Ltd remains the company's property until full payment for the work is received.

Other suppliers, such as photographers, will have their own copyright conditions and it is the responsibility of the client to adhere to these.

You Logo Ltd does not charge VAT.

t 020 1234 1234 | **f** 020 1234 1235 | www.yourwebsite.co.uk
Your House, Your Road, Your Town, Your City, AB1 2CD

Appendix 5

Example invoice

t 020 1234 1234 | f 020 1234 1235 | www.yourwebsite.co.uk
Your House, Your Road, Your Town, Your City, AB1 2CD

YOUR
LOGO

Your Client
The High Street,
Another Town,
AB1 2YZ

10th December 2011

Invoice No: 1234567890

Invoice

TEMPLATE DESIGN
Purchase Order number: TR172   £500.00
Delivered 1 December 2011

Payment within 30 days please   **Total:**   **£500.00**
Cheques payable to **Your Logo Ltd**   **Carriage:**
BACS payments to: **Balance due:**   **£500.00**
Your Logo Ltd at Barclays Bank plc
Account No. 12345678
Sort code: 11-22-33

VAT no: 123456789
NI no: AB 12 34 56C